CONTENTS مُحْتَوَيات ألْكِتاب

Part One: Nine Letters

Introduction ألْمُقَدِمَة III
Important Notes 1
Chapter 1: daal: دال 2
Chapter 2: 'elif: ألَف 6
Chapter 3: waaw: واو 8
The sounds of waaw واو 8
Chapter 4: raa': راء 12
Chapter 5: zaay: زاي 17
Chapter 6: dhaal: ذال 20
Chapter 7: Taa': طاء 22
Chapter 8: yaa': ياء 28
The sounds of yaa' ياء 28
The prefix ye: يَـ 36
The calling device yaa: يا 38
Chapter 9: laam: لام 39
Punctuations in Arabic 39
The l+aa shape: لا 43
Chart of the nine learned letters and their shapes 48

Part Two: Nine Symbols

Chapter 1: The three short vowels:
    kesreh: كَسْرَة 50
    Demeh: ضَمَة 50
    fetHeh: فَتْحَة 50
Chapter 2:
    no vowel: sikoon سِكون 52
    double letter: sheddeh شَدَّة 53
    meddeh: مَدَّة 54
Chapter 3:
    'elif meqSooreh ألَف مَقْصورة 55
    tenween: تَنْوين 56
Chapter 4: hemzeh: هَمزة 57
Chapter 5: Numbers 1-20 64
Summary of the Nine Arabic Symbols 65
Summary of all Learned Letters and Symbols 66
Practice Test of Parts One and Two: Translate to Arabic Letters 67

Part Three: Six More Letters

Chapter 1: baa': باء 70
Chapter 2: meem: ميم 74
Chapter 3: haa': هاء 79
Chapter 4: noon: نون 84
Chapter 5: jeem: جيم 90

Chapter 6: seen: سين 96
Chapter 7: Numbers 21-100 100
Chart of the Six Learned Letters in Part Three and their Shapes.................................. 101
Summary of the Arabic Vowels and Six other Symbols 101
Practice Test: Translate these sounds and words into Arabic letters 102

Part Four: Seven More Letters

Chapter 1: taa': تاء 105
The taa' merbooTeh تاء مَرْبوطَة 108
Chapter 2: faa': فاء 112
Chapter 3: kaaf: كاف 116
Chapter 4: Daad: ضاد 122
Chapter 5: Aeyn: عَين 126
Chapter 6: sheen: شين 134
Chapter 7: Haa': حاء 138
Chapter 8: Arabic numbers: 100 – 1000000: 142

Part Five: The Last Six Letters

Chapter 1: thaa': ثاء 145
Chapter 2: khaa': خاء 150
Chapter 3: Saad: صاد 157
Chapter 4: Zaa': ظاء 164
Synonyms & Homonyms 167
Chapter 5: gheyn: غَين 170
Chapter 6: qaaf: قاف 177
Rules to divide Arabic words into syllables 183
Practice test of Part Five: Translate 184
List of the Arabic alphabet in their actual order 185
Chart of the Arabic alphabet + nine symbols and their different shapes 186

About this textbook:
- ✓ The author is a Linguist who dissected both English and Arabic.
- ✓ This book caters to the specific needs of English speakers.
- ✓ With meticulous transliteration, students begin to read from the first day of class.
- ✓ Arabic vowels, consonants, and nine Arabic symbols are dissected.
- ✓ Essential rules that govern the structure of Arabic words are discovered.
- ✓ No other methodology has 40+ original learning features in one program.
- ✓ It contains 800+ cognates.
- ✓ It is a class-tested approach.
- ✓ It works with or without a teacher.
- ✓ You also need *Spoken Arabic for English Speakers* by Camilia Sadik.

INTRODUCTION ألْمُقَدِمَة

The Arabic Alphabet for English Speakers

Instructions & Learning Features

1. Direct Instructions: تعليمات ألْكِتاب مَكْتوبَة مُباشَرَةً في بدايَة كُل دَرْس جَديد
Teachers do not need a teacher's guide because there are direct instructions before the start of each lesson in this entire book. All explanations are written in English, and the Arabic words are written both in Arabic letters and in English transliterations, as in (Madrid: med·reed′ مَدْريد). If any teacher doesn't agree with using transliteration, he or she has the choice of ignoring the transliteration and teaching only from the Arabic text available in this book. Some teachers insist on having a teacher's guide; and this long introduction is their teacher's guide.

2. Dots inside words, italic letters, stress marks: مَعْنى ألْنقاط داخِل ألْكَلِمات ومَعنى ألْحِروف ألْمائِلَة وَعَلامَة ألْتَشْديد
   1. All words in this book are divided into syllables as in, (radio: raad·yōo رادْيو).
   2. All silent letters are italicized like as in, (the rice: ′el·ruzz ألْرُزّ).
   3. Stress marks are placed on every stressed syllable, as in (Cincinnati: sin·si·naa′·tee).

3. Unique transliteration: كِتابَة ألْعَرَبِيَة بِحروف إنْجِليزيَة
Using the precise transliteration in this book is one choice; the other choice is using the Arabic letters that are also available; they are written next to the transliteration like this (te·li·foon′ تَلِفون). The author transferred the Arabic alphabet to English letters. Using transliteration, students begin to speak Arabic from the first day of class. They also learn the 28 Arabic letters and the nine symbols within weeks. Transliteration is only a step and when finishing with the alphabet book, students will directly read any other Arabic text.

4. Meticulous sounds' translation: دِقَة تَرْجَمَة ألْصَوْت وَالألِف ألْمَقْصورة كَمَثَل
Arabic sounds are meticulously translated; it took the author five long years discovering and class testing to produce two unique books; see how the English "aw" as in "law" is introduced for the first time ever to represent the sound of ى as in moo′·see·qaw: موسيقى.

5. Six capital letters inside words: طاء، ضاد، عين، حاء، صاد، ظاء
Don't be discouraged when you see English capital letters inside words, as in ribaaT رباط. There aren't enough English letters to represent all the 28 Arabic letters; hence, six English capital letters are used to represent six Arabic sounds that do not have an equivalent letter sound in English. The capitol "T" represents the Arabic letter (Taa': طاء) as in (kilowatt: kee′·loo·waaT كيلو واط), a capital "D" represents the (Daad: ضاد) as in (Riyadh: ri·yaaD′ رياض), a capital "A" represent the (Aeyn: عين) as in (Ae·re·bee′ عَرَبي), a capital "H" represent the (Haa': حاء) as in (He·bee′·bee حَبيبي), a capital "S" represents the (Saad: صاد) as in (bus: baaS باص) and a capital "Z" represents the (Zaa' ظاء) as in (meH·fooZ′ مَحْفوظ).
   1. T ط
      The capital "T" ط represents a slightly different sound of a "t." Examples of words that contain the "T" sound are (kilowatt: kee·lōo·waaT كيلو واط), (pants: ben·Te·loon بَنْطَلون), and (bottle: bu·Tul بُطُل), You will need to hear this Arabic sound to learn it.
   2. A ع
      The capital "A" ع represents a slightly different sound from the English "a." Examples of words that contain "A" ع are (Saudi: si·Aoo·dee سِعودي), (Iraq: Ai·raaq عِراق), and (street: shaa·riA شارع). You will need to hear this Arabic sound to learn it.
   3. q ق

III

The "q" قاف sounds slightly different from the English "k." Examples of words that contain "q" ق are (Iraq: Ai·raaq عِراق), (hotel: fin·diq فُنْدق), and (market: sooq سوق). You will need to hear this Arabic sound to learn it.

4. S ص

The capital "S" ص represents a slightly different sound from the English "s"; it is close to the English "s" is "sum." Examples of words that contain the "S" صاد sound are (glass: klaaS كُلاص), (bus: baaS باص), (Somalia: 'el·Sōo·maal أَلصومال). You will need to hear this Arabic sound to learn it.

5. D ض

The capital "D" ض represents a slightly different sound from the English "d." Examples of a word that contain the "D" sound are (eggs: beyD بَيض) and (white: 'eb·yeD أَبْيَض). You will need to hear this Arabic sound to learn it.

6. Z ظ

The capital "Z" ظ represents a slightly different sound from the Arabic (D ض) and to many Arabic speakers, it is difficult to tell their sounds apart. The good news is that the Z occurs in about 38 words. In Egyptian dialect, this difficultly is solved because a plain "z" sound is used to represent this sound. Examples of words that contain the (Zaa' ظاء) sound are (meH·fooZ' مَحْفوظ), (clean: ne·Zeef نَظيف'), (great: Ae·Zeem' عَظيم) and the letter (Zaa' ظاء).

6. (dh ذ) and (th ث)

In this book, the (th ث) symbol is equivalent to the sound of (th ث) as in (thermos: thir·mus ثُرْمُس) and the (dh ذ) is equivalent to the sound of (dh ذ) as in (Heather: he·dher هَذَر).

7. There are no letters equivalent to p, v, o, ch, hard g, and si:

Arabic does not have letters equivalent to the English p, v, long ō, ch as in chips, hard g, and si as in television. However, Arabic speakers may say the "p" in "piano" and write (bee·yaa·nōo بيانو). Similarly, Arabic speakers may say the "v" in "oven" and write ('ōo·fin أوفِن). They may say the "ch" in "chips" and write (jibs جِبْس). They may say the hard "g" in "garage" and write (ka·raaj كَراج). They do say the long "ō" sound in "radiō" and write (raa·dyoo راديو). Arabic uses the "z" for the "si" sound as in (television: ta·la·fiz·yōon تَلْفِزيون) and they do that both in spoken and in written Arabic.

8. Right to left: كِتابَة أَلْعَرَبِية مِن أَلْيَسار إِلى أَلْيَمين

Arabic is written and read from right to left←:

9. Cursive only: أَلْحُروف أَلْعَرَبِيَة مُتَّصِلَة (مَزج)

Arabic is written only in cursive; even in print, Arabic is in cursive. Like the English cursive, Arabic letters are connected to each other. However, six of the Arabic letters are not connected to each other but they are connected to other letters from their right side only. They are selfish letters because they receive connection, but they do not give it; they connect to the preceding but not to the following letters.

10. Understanding Arabic and English vowels is essential: فِهم حروف أَلْعِلَة أَلْعَرَبِية وَألإِنْجِليزِية مُهِم جِداً

English vowels are a, e, i, o, u, sometimes y as in sky, and sometimes w as in few. Unlike Arabic, English uses the same letter for the short and for the long sound of a vowel. For instance, English uses the same letter "e" to represent the short ĕ sound as in "set" and the long ē sound as in "seat". Unlike English, Arabic has three letters for the long vowels and three distinct symbols for the short vowels. The short vowels are not letters; they are small strokes or blips written above or below the consonants; their name is He·re·kaat' حَرَكات. Understanding the vowels in both languages is very necessary because vowels rule a language. Luckily, the author of this program dissected the vowels in both languages and has written books about them.

11. The three long Arabic vowels: أَلِف واو ياء
In this book, the three Arabic long vowels are represented in (aa أَلِف) that sound like the "a" in "cat", the (ee ياء) that sounds like the "ee" in "meet", and the (oo واو) that sounds like the "oo" in "boot".
   1. The 'elif: أَلِف
      The long Arabic vowel "aa" is called 'elif أَلِف and it is normally pronounced like the "a" in "father" but changes to like the "a" in "man" when next to an "emphatic" consonant. Emphatic consonants are: (H, A, D, S, Z حروف ألإطْباق).
      The 'elif meqSooreh: أَلِف مَقْصورَة is a weaker version of the 'elif sound; it sounds like the English "aw" in "law" and it occurs only at the end of Arabic words. The symbol given to it in this book is "aw" as in music: mōo'·see·qaw: موسيقى.

   2. The waaw: واو
      The long vowel "oo" is called waaw واو and it sounds like the "oo" in "boot". In a few words, it sounds like the long vowel ō as in bōat. The few words are mainly derived from English or other foreign languages. Examples are: raad'·yōo, sti·ryōo', te·li·fōon', 'ōo'·fin, 'el·bōom', 'ōor·laan·dōo, 'ōo'·haa·yōo, dee'·trōoyt, dōo'·laar, bee'·yaa·nōo, te·le·fiz·yōon', rōob, kaar'·tōon, shōo'·kōo·laa·taa, mōo'·see·qaw, meA·ke·rōo'·nee, bananas: mōoz موز, and plums: khōokh خوخ.
      It is said that the word (bananas: mōoz موز) is derived from the Persian language. Just like the "w" in "water", when the letter و is at the beginning of a word, it sounds like the consonant "w" و as in: (Washington: waa·shin·Tin واشِنْطِن) and (one: waa·Hid واحِد).

   3. The yaa': ياء
      The long Arabic vowel "ee" is called yaa' ياء and it is normally pronounced like the "ee" in "meet" but it stops being a vowel and it changes to the sound of "y"; when at the beginning of words or syllables, as in Japan: yaa·baan يابان. Just like the English "y" in "yes", the "y" as in (bey'·root بيْروت) and (lemons: ley'·moon لَيْمون) becomes a consonant. However, the "y" is silent in words derived from English or other languages, as in (wave: we*y*f), and (microwave: maay'·krōo·we*y*f). The "aay" occurs at the end of a few words or syllables, sounds like the long English "i" as in (maay'·krōo·we*y*f) and as in (zaay زاي).

12. The three short Arabic vowels: فَتْحَة ضَمَة كَسْرَة
The three Arabic short vowels are represented in (e فَتْحَة) that sounds like the short English "e" in "set", (i كَسْرَة) that sounds like the short English "i" in "sit", and the (u ضَمَة) that sounds like the "u" in "put". The short Arabic vowels are not letters; instead, they are tiny blips or strokes written above or below consonants.
   1. The fetHeh: فَتْحَة is represented with an "e" in this book, and it sounds like the short English vowel ĕ as in "set." When not stressed it sounds like a schwa, like the weak "e" sound in "brother". The fetHeh: فَتْحَة is not a letter but it is a blip written <u>above</u> consonants.

   2. The Demeh: ضَمَة is a short vowel represented with a "u" in this book, and it sounds like the English "u" in "put". This Arabic short vowel has a strong sound, and it is also a blip written <u>above</u> consonants.

   3. The kesreh: كَسْرَة is represented with an "i" in this book, and it sounds like short English vowel "ĭ" in "sit". When stressed at the end of a word or a syllable, it sounds like the "i" in "ski." It is also a blip, but it is the only vowel written <u>below</u> the consonants.

13. Representing the fetHeh فَتْحَة sound with "e" not "a": تَرْجَمَة صَوت أَلْفَتْحَة
Too many Arabic words that contain the short Arabic vowel fetHeh فَتْحَة have been incorrectly transliterated or translated to English. The "e" should have been used, not the "a" to represent the sound of the Arabic fetHeh فَتْحَة. The prefix "Al", meaning "the" is widely used; it often prefixes Arabic proper nouns, especially names of places; an example is Al-Jazirah أَلْجَزِيرَة (Arabic: "The Island"). The "a", which is the fetHeh فَتْحَة should have been an "e" in Al-Jazirah because it sounds like a short English "e" not "a"; it should be spelled (El-Jezeereh). The precise sound of the fetHeh فَتْحَة is like the short English "e", not "a". In the beginning of her career, the author used "a" for the sound of the fetHeh فَتْحَة and her students would spell words like (thank you: shukr<u>a</u>n شُكْراً) as (shukr<u>aa</u>n شُكْران) confusing the "a" with the short vowel "a" in English.

14. meddeh مَدَّة sounds like the short vowel (ă آ) as in (Adam آدَم)
The med′·deh مَدَّة is a symbol that sits above the 'elif أَلِف and together they sound like the English short vowel ă, like the first "a" in (Adam: آدَم) and as in (Ann آن). It also occurs inside words at the beginning of a syllables, as in (Koran قُرْآن). The meddeh مَدَّة occurs at the beginning of words or syllables and it is a minor symbol because it is in a limited number of words.

15. Schwa صَوت حَرف أَلْعِلَة أَلْضَعِيف
A schwa is a name given to a weak sound of any English vowel. English dictionaries use this symbol ə to represent a schwa sound. A schwa sound is like the "a" sound in (beggər: beggər). In Arabic, a schwa sound is as in (fish: semək: semək سَمَك) It is usually the short Arabic vowels "e" "فَتْحَة" and "i" "كَسْرَة" that can sound like a schwa. The Arabic schwa is mainly represented by an "i" "kesreh" in Egyptian dialect ('iswid: black أَسْوِد) and by an "e" "fetHeh" in the Gulf dialect ('eswed: black أَسْوَد).

16. No vowel sound: sikoon سِكون
The word si·koon′ سِكون literally means "no sound." The sikoon سِكون is a tiny circle written above a letter to assert the no vowel existence, as it being above the (d دْ). When there is no vowel between two consonants, there can be a (sikoon سِكون), as in (film: film فِلْم). Sometimes, a sikoon can be at the end of words, as in (mother: 'um أُمْ). What English calls a consonant blend; Arabic calls it a sikoon سِكون. Examples of sikoon in words are: (Madrid: med·reed′ مَدْرِيد) and (food: 'ekl أَكْل).

17. Stressed syllable: أَلْمَقطع أَلْمُشَدَد
A syllable that contains any of the three long Arabic vowels (aa, oo, ee) attracts the stress to itself, as in (Beirut: bey·root′), (chair: kur·see′), and (book: ki·taab′). Otherwise, Arabic words are normally stressed on the first syllable, as in (sugar: suk′·kar).
  1. Stress marks: عَلامَة أَلْتَشْدِيد موجودة في كَلِمات إِلْكِتاب كُلّها
     A stress mark is placed at the end of each stressed syllable in all the words in this book, as in: (fe·laa′·fil فَلافِل).
  2. A rule to know the stress in a syllable: قاعدة أَلْتَشْدِيد عَلى أَلْمَقْطَع
     This is a concrete simple rule to place a stress mark on a syllable. The stress is on the first long vowel in a word, as in (physics: feez′·yaa′ فيزياء). If there is no long vowel in a word the stress is on the first syllable, as in (sugar: suk′·ker سُكَّر).

18. hem′·zeh هَمْزة as in (physics: feez′·yaa′ فيزياء):
The name of this symbol is hem′·zeh هَمْزة and it sounds like the sound of the glottal stop in the English word 'Uh 'Oh! It is most known in Arabic as the letter that rides on long vowels. The English symbol given to the hemzeh هَمْزة in this book is an apostrophe, as in 'e·laa·skeh ألاسْكا. There is an ongoing debate whether the hamzah هَمْزة is or is not a letter. However, it may be considered a letter when it can stand alone, as in (physics: feez′·yaa′ فيزياء). The rest of the time, the hemzeh هَمْزة occurs riding on the

long vowels and thus it may not be considered a letter. When the hemzeh rides on the long vowels, it suppresses their sounds; it makes them silent and then we only hear the hemzeh هَمْزَة sound. The followings are the hemzeh هَمْزَة positions alone and when riding above or below the three long Arabic vowels like this أ, إ, ؤ and ىء.

19. The silent 'elif under the hemzeh: أَلِف صَامِتِة تحت ألْهَمْزَة
Whenever you see an 'e أ at the beginning of a word or a syllable, it is spelled with a silent (aa أ) before it. For instance, (food: 'ekl أَكل) is spelled aa'ekl أَكل and the 'el as in 'el·Hi·saab is spelled (aa'el·Hi·saab ألْحِساب) in Arabic. The hemzeh rides on the 'elif and it suppresses its sound.

20. Sun Letters: ألْحروف ألْشَمْسِيَة
Fifteen of the Arabic letters are called Sun Letters, and they are:
سين، شين، صاد، راء، تاء، طاء، لام، جيم، نون، دال، ذال، ثاء، زاي، ضاد، ظاء.

t ت	r ر	S ص	sh ش	s س
d د	n ن	j ج	l ل	T ط
Z ظ	D ض	z ز	th ث	dh ذ

21. Silent L ل before a sun letter: أللام الصامت قبل الحرف الشمسي
The "l" in 'el ألـ becomes silent when followed by a sun letter, as in ('el·soob ألْسوب), ('el·shaay ألْشاي), ('el·Se·HeeH ألْصَحيح), ('el·ruzz ألْرُزّ), ('el·tek·see ألْتَكْسي), ('el·Taa·lib ألْطالِب), ('el·le·dheed ألْلَذيذ), ('el·je·meel ألْجَميل), ('el·naas ألْناس), ('el·di·jaaj ألْدِجاج), ('el·dhe·heb ألْذَهَب), ('el·thoom ألْثوم), ('el·zee·braa ألْزيبرا), ('el·De·meh ألْضَمَة), and ('el·Zaa' ألْظاء). If not followed by a sun letter, the 'e in 'el is silent and the "l" has a sound, as in ('el·baab ألْباب) and as in 'el plus any other letter that is not a sun letter, including the vowels ('el·'ōo·fin ألأوفِن).

22. sheddeh شَدَّة for double consonants:
The shed'·deh شَدَّة is a tiny symbol that goes above a consonant to assert the existence of a double consonant, as in (rice: ruzz رزّ). Instead of doubling the consonants, the sheddeh شَدَّة is placed on the consonant and takes the place of the second consonant.

23. The feminine suffix (eh ـة) or (et ـة) ألتاء ألْمَربوطَة
Most countries and cities' names are expressed in a feminine gender. Most of which end in the suffix (et ـة). This suffix is written with an "et" but pronounced "eh". i.e., the (et ـة) is pronounced (eh ـة) as in (Syria: sooryet سوريَة), sounding like (Syria: sooryeh سوريَة). The Arabic words for "country" is (dewleh دَوْلَة) and city is (medeeneh مَدينَة) and both end with (et ـة) that sounds like (eh ـة). Both words are in a feminine form. Think of a country's name being feminine as mother earth. The suffix is pronounced as (eh ـة) or (et ـة) depending on the word that follows it or if it isn't followed by any words. When it's followed by an owner, it is pronounced like "et" as in: (Sam being the owner of a car: siy·yaa·ret Sam). There is more about the taa' merbooTeh ألتاء ألْمَربوطَة that is explained in the book titled *Spoken Arabic for English Speakers by Camilia Sadik*.

24. The tenween تَنْوين as in شُكْراً:
The ten·ween' تَنْوين is an ending (suffix) that can have three different sounds. The first sound is like the "en" as in "taken" and in the Arabic word (thank you: shuk·ren شُكْراً). The other two sounds are "un" that sounds like the "un" in (a book: ki·taa·bun كِتابٌ) and the "in" sound as in (ki·taa·bin كِتابٍ). The "un" and "in" endings involve the grammatical structure of sentences, not just words. It is best to study them at advanced levels of Arabic in the future. In this book, we are mainly concerned with the grammar inside the words and in simple sentences. Hence, "en" ending as in shuk·ren شُكْراً is the only one we will be studying here. When first hearing the "en" sound as in شُكْراً, one assumes that it is spelled with an "n ن."

Introduction

However, there is no "n ن" in these tenween endings. Instead, there is a double blip sitting above the 'elif as in shuk·ren شُكْراً or above the end isolated hemzeh like this ءً as in (please: ri·jaa'··'en رِجاءً). Notice that most of these words are adverbs. Learn the tenween in these words:

thanks	shuk'·ra*a*en	شُكْراً
you're welcome	Aef'·wa*a*en	عَفْواً
very	ji'·da*a*en	جِداً
please (not v.)	ri·jaa'··'en	رِجاءً
a lot	ke·thee'·ra*a*en	كَثيراً
in the morning	Se·baa'·Ha*a*en	صَباحاً
tomorrow	ghe'·den	غَداً
always	daa'·'i·ma*a*en	دائِماً
in the evening	me·saa·aa'en	مَساءً
nighttime	ley'·la*a*en	لَيلاً
a little	qe·lee'·la*a*en	قَليلاً
first of all	'ew'·we·la*a*en	أَوَلاً

25. Summary of the Arabic vowels and other symbols:

de: دَ   daa: دا   du: دُ   doo: دو

di: دِ   dee: دي   -den: دً   dd: دّ

dl: دْ   aw: ى   ă=aa: آ   ': ء

26. The prefix (the: 'el ألـ)

The *aa*'el ألـ means "the" and it is a prefix in Arabic, as in (the door: 'elbaab ألْباب) Being a prefix means it attaches to the word that follows it. The *aa*'el ألـ can mean "the" and it can simply be a part of a person's surname or a part of a country's name. Some countries' names like (Algeria: ألْجَزائِر) begin with *aa*'el, some can't take an *aa*'el like (Palestine: فَلَسْطين), and others may take an *aa*'el ألـ only to mean "the" (The Gulf: ألْخَليج). The 'elif أ in *aa*'el ألـ is silent because the hemzeh هَمْزَة riding on it suppresses its sound.

27. The prefix (and: we وَ) pronounced (wi وِ):
(we + 'el + sun letter) sound like (wi + 'el + sun letter) as in (and the rice: we'elruzz وَرُزّ) sounding like (wiruzz وِرُزّ). But, (we + 'el + other than a sun letter) sounds like (wil) as in the change from (we'elbaab وَلْباب) to (wilbaab وِلْباب).

28. Letters have names, sounds, and shapes: أَسْماء ألْحُروف ألْعَرَبِيَة وأَصِواتِها وأَشْكالِها
All Arabic letters are first introduced with their Arabic letter name, the English symbol given in this book to each letter, and then its four shapes are presented. For instance, the name of the second Arabic letter is (baa' باء) and the English symbol given to it in this book is (b), and its four shapes from right to left are: ب ـب ـبـ بـ

29. Letter's shapes: لِلْحَرف ألْعَرَبي أَرْبَعَة أَشْكال
All Arabic letters, except for six, have four shapes and they are a beginning, middle, end, and isolated (detached) shape. Nearly all four shapes are basically the same, but the attachments and the endings make them look different. For instance, the Arabic letter Taa' طاء is given the symbol of a capital "T" and is written in these four ways from right to left: ط ـط ـطـ طـ

30. About this Teaching Methodology: عَن طَريقَة ألتعليم في هَذا أَلْكِتاب
It is rare for a teacher to have dissected both Arabic and English. The developer of this unique teaching/learning methodology is a native-Arabic speaker, and she spent five long years dissecting Arabic and then 15 more years dissecting English.

31. Following instructions: أَهَمِيَة إِتِّباع تَعليمات أَلْكِتاب
Teachers need to warn students that this easy method is different and true learning relies immensely on following instruction and following the four simple learning steps explained before each lesson. Lessons are introduced step-by-step, and they are cumulative; each lesson adds more to the previous ones.

32. Four learning steps: خَطَوات ألتعَلُّم أَرْبَعَة
The following four steps are a summary of the easy steps given before each lesson to teach a new letter:
- ❶ Learning Step One: Find, utter, and trace on top of the letter (b ب) as in the (ب in بَيت):
- ❷ Learning Step Two: Don't write yet, first read aloud these sounds (phonics) five times per page:
- ❸ Step Three: Practice writing these sounds or words or phrases:
- ❹ Step Four: Pick the correct shape of the learned letter to fill in blanks:

33. Why should you read and speak aloud: أَهَمِيَة ألْقِراءَة بِصَوت عالِ
1. To hear your own mistakes and learn from them.
2. To hear sound and improve your pronunciation.
3. To practice alone, you don't have to have another person listening to you.
4. To gain confidence and fluency in speaking, reading, and then writing.
5. To have this class-tested methodology work for you.
6. Because more memory comes from using more senses, as in hearing the sounds.
7. Because this method is different, and it doesn't work without uttering the sounds.
8. Because it's not enough to think a sentence, you need to say it.
9. Because speaking a language is about making sounds.

34. Specifically for English speakers: تَعليم أَلْعَرَبِيَة هنا هُوَ تَحديداً لمتكلمي أَلإِنْجِليزية
Using both books by *Camilia Sadik*; students begin to read Arabic from the first day of class. They begin to read immediately using English transliteration. From the other book, students speak Arabic from the first day of class. This program caters to the specific needs of English speakers, and it is comprehensive; it covers all aspects of Arabic relevant to a new learner.

35. Unique learning methodology: طَريقَة تَعْليم فَريدَة مِن نَوعها
Over 40 new features and learning techniques are used to make learning easy and possible. Explanations followed by immediate practice to learn the Arabic vowels, the consonants, consonant blends, double letters, schwa, the Arabic hemzeh, how to divide Arabic words into syllables, which syllables to be stressed, silent letters, and a one of its kind learning methodology that requires no forced memorization or flash cards.

Sample Rule: Arabic words are normally stressed on the first long vowel in a word, as in (Baghdad: begh·daad' بَغْداد) and as in (Denmark: de·nee'·maark دَنيمارْك). If a word doesn't contain a long vowel, it is stressed on the first short vowel, as in (Damascus: di'·meshq دِمَشْق).

36. Grouping of words: تَجْميع أَلْكَلِمات أَلْمُتَشابِهَة سَوِيَة
All words of a similar pattern are grouped together, divided into syllables, each silent letter is *italicized*. The words are prepared for the students to simply read and learn. Unlike traditional teaching that presents students with one or a few examples, the author collects 10 to 30 examples or more and hands them to students.

37. Class-tested, effective new approach: طَريقَة أَلْتَعْليم فَعّالَة وجديدة وهي مُجَرَبَة في أَرْبع ْجامِعات أَمْريكِيَة
Professor Camilia Sadik class-tested her methodology while teaching English speakers in four colleges in San Diego, California. With this class-tested, effective approach to learning, most master the Arabic alphabet in fifteen or thirty days, learning either one or two letters per day.

38. A book for all: كِتاب لِكافة أَلأعمار وَأَلْمُسْتَوَيات مَعَ مُعَلِّم أَو بِدون مُعَلِّم
Students may learn from this book with or without a teacher. This book also accommodates diverse needs in one classroom. English speakers from multilevel, multicultural backgrounds and from any age group can learn to speak, read, and write in Arabic in one classroom. Not only do students learn, but also, they remember what they learn. Students retain what they learn without forced memorization, but through logical explanations and reading the practice lessons aloud.

39. More features: مَزيد مِن أَلْمَزايا
This book is easy to read, the language is in plain, spoken Arabic. The English transliteration used is very precise and consistent when it corresponds to each Arabic sound. All short vowels and other Arabic symbols are written above or below Arabic letters. This book is in large print. See a complete chart of the alphabet at the end of the alphabet book. Notice the silent letters being italicized, words being divided into syllables, the stressed syllables marked with a stress mark. See the consistency of sound corresponding in the following examples:

Cincinnati:	sin·si·naa′·tee	سِنْسِيناتي
Beirut:	bey′·root	بَيْروت
falafel:	fe·laa′·fil	فلافِل
kabob:	ke·baab′	كَباب
the market:	′il·sooq′	إلْسوق
in English:	bi′el·′in·ki·lee·zee	بأَلإنْكْليزي

40. Syllables: كَلِمات إلْكِتاب كُلها مُقَسَمَة إلى مَقاطِع
This book teaches over 3000 words, and they are all divided into syllables: sin·si·naa′·tee سِنْسِيناتي

41. Stress marks: عَلامَة أَلْتَشْديد موجودة في كَلِمات إلْكِتاب كُلها
A stress mark is placed at the end of each stressed syllable in all 3000 words: fe·laa′·fil فلافِل

42. Order of introducing each letter: أَلْتَسَلْسُل أَلَذي تُقَدَم به أَلْحِروف مُخَطط لَه
Learning the alphabet in this book is a process. The order of the letters and words given is not random. This system is especially designed to make learning easier for English speakers. Therefore, following the order of the lessons given in this book and following all the instructions is exceedingly important.

43. Cognates: أَلإسْتِفادة مِن إسْتِخْدام حَوالي 800 كَلِمة مُتَشابِهَة
In this book, over 800 cognates are used to make learning easier and smoother: kee′·loo·waaT كيلو واط

44. Silent letters: أَلْحُروف أَلْصامِتَة مائِلَة
All silent letters throughout the entire book are italicized: ′el·aa′·ur′·dun أَلأرْدُن.

45. Symbols and short vowels: إستخدام أَلْحَركات في كَلِمات أَلْكِتاب كُله
All the short vowels are placed below or above the consonants in each Arabic word in this book; all other symbols are also placed on or next to words: أُم, سَيّارَة, دائِماً

46. The book *Spoken Arabic for English Speakers by Camilia Sadik*: أَلْعَرَبِيَة أَلْمَحْكِيَة لِمُتَكَلِّمي أْلإنْكِليزِيَة

This book caters to the specific needs of English speakers. Because of the precise transliteration students begin to speak Arabic instantly and from the first day of class. Vowels, consonants, nine Arabic symbols are all dissected. Essential rules that govern the structure of the Arabic words are discovered. The methodology is unique; no other methodology has over 40 new features and learning techniques in one program. It teaches sentence patterns, grouping of words, and conjugating of verbs. As a result, students learn a method to teach themselves indefinitely. In addition, each learned word is presented in four major Arabic dialects for the student to choose his or her desired dialect. It is a class-tested approach, for all ages, and it works with or without a teacher.

47. The Four Major Arabic Dialects: أَللَهَجات أَلْعَرَبِية أَلأَرْبَعَة أَلرئيسِيَة

Arabic speakers in 22 Arabian countries speak a countless number of dialects. In addition to the formal form of Arabic (فصحى), there are three other major dialects spoken in three major regions in the Middle East, and they are:
   1. The Egyptian dialect أَللَهَجَة أَلْمَصْرِيَة
   2. The Gulf area dialect أَللَهَجَة الخَلِيجِيَة
   3. The Mediterranean dialect لَهْجَة أَلْبَحْر أَلأبْيَض أَلْمُتَوَسِط

48. The Egyptian Dialect: أَللَهَجَة أَلْمَصْرِيَة

The Egyptian dialect is the most understood in all Arabian countries. This is due to the movie industry that flourished in Egypt since the 1950s and Arabic speakers watched Egyptian movies and they still do. If one is trying to learn spoken Arabic, it is safer to learn the Egyptian dialect. In this spoken Arabic book, the author picked the words that are most understood in every Arabian country, mostly Egyptian dialect is used. At the end of Part One and Part Two of this book, there are charts of the learned words presented the four major dialects. From the charts, you may select words you wish to learn from any of the four dialects.

49. A list of the Arabian countries and their capitols: أَلْدِوَل أَلْعَرَبِيَة وَعَواصِمَها
   1. Gulf region: أَلْدِوَل الخَلِيجِيَة
      Iraq: أَلْعِراق →Baghdad: بَغْداد   Kuwait: أَلْكُوَيت →Kuwait: أَلْكُوَيت
      Saudi Arabia: أَلْسعودِيَة →Riyadh: أَلْرياض   Bahrain: أَلْبَحرَين →Manama: أَلْمَنامَة
      Oman: عُمان →Muscat: مَسْقَط   UAE: أَلإمارات →Abu Dhabi: أَبو ظَبي
      Dubai: دُبَي →Dubai: دُبَي   Qatar: قَطَر →Doha: أَلدوحَة

   2. The Mediterranean region: دِوَل أَلْبَحْر أَلأبْيَض أَلْمُتَوَسِط
      Lebanon: لُبْنان →Beirut: بَيْروت   Syria: سورِيَة →Damascus: دِمَشق
      Jordan: أَلأَرْدُن →Amman: عَمّان   Palestine: فِلِسْطين →Jerusalem: أَلْقُدْس
      Yemen: أَلْيَمَن →Sana: صَنْعاء   Aden: عَدَن →Aden: عَدَن

   3. Egypt and Parts of Africa: أَلْدِوَل أَلْقَرِيبة مِن مِصر
      Egypt: مِصر →Cairo: أَلْقاهِرَة   Libya: لِيبيا →Tripoli: طَرَبُلس
      Tunisia: تونِس →Tunis: تونِس   Algeria: أَلْجَزائر →Algeria: أَلْجَزائر
      Morocco: أَلْمَغْرب →Rabat: أَلرباط   Sudan: أَلْسودان →Khartoum: أَلْخَرْطوم
      Somalia: أَلْصومال →Mogadishu: مَقْديشو   Djibouti: جيبوتي →Djibouti: جيبوتي
      Mauritania: موريتانيا →Nouakchott: نَواكْشوط

Introduction

50. In the spoken Arabic book, you can choose your desired dialect from the charts at the end of each part of the book. In the charts, learned words are listed in the four major dialects, like this:

Learned Words in the Four Major Dialects

You may choose your dialect and plug in the words chosen to use in the lessons you want to learn:

Learned Word	Egypt	Mediterranean	Gulf	FuSHaw
haa·dhaa هذا	daa دا	hey·dhaa هَيْدا	haa·dhaa هذا	haa·dhaa هذا
sooq سوق	soo' سوء	soo' سوء	sook سوك	sooq سوق
kitaab كِتاب	ki·taab كِتاب	kitaab كِتاب	kitaab كِتاب	ki·taab كِتاب
shu·baak شُباك	shi·baak شِباك	shi·baak شِباك	shu·baak شُباك	shu·baak شُباك
'elaan ألآن	dil we·'e·tee دِلْوَءْتي	he·laa هَلا	he·seh هَسَه	'el·aan ألآن

Learned Verbs in Four Major Arabic Dialects

Learned Verbs	Egyptian	Mediterranean	Gulf	FuSHa
yenaam ينام	yinaam ينام	yenaam ينام	yenaam ينام	yenaam يَنام
yejeeb يجيب	yigeeb يكيب	yejeeb يجيب	yejeeb يجيب	yejlub يَجْلُب
yeshoof يشوف	yishoof يِشوف	yeshoof يشوف	yeshoof يشوف	yeraw يَرى
yerooH يروح	yirooH يِروح	yerooH يروح	yerooH يروح	yedhheb يَذهَب
yesewwee يسَوّي	yiAmil يَعْمِل	yesaawwee يساوي	yesewwee يسَوّي	yeAmel يَعْمَل
yimshee يِمْشي	yimshee يِمْشي	yimshee يِمْشي	yimshee يِمْشي	yemshee يَمْشي

▶There is much more to learn within each new lesson in this book.

Books by the author Camilia Sadik كُتُب لِلمُؤَلِفَة كاميليا صادق

Arabic Books: كُتُب بِٱلْعَرِيبِة لِلمؤَلِفة
1. *Spoken Arabic for English Speakers*: This book teaches spoken Arabic to beginners.
2. *The Arabic Alphabet for English Speakers*: This book teaches the 28 Arabic letters and nine symbols.
3. *English for Arabic Speakers*: This book teaches spoken English to Arabic speakers. However, it's a great resource for English speakers to learn commonly used Arabic words in both languages. For instance, chapter one contains the names of the items that exist in a home both in Arabic and in English.

➤You also need *Spoken Arabic for English Speakers by Camilia Sadik*: أَلْعَرَبِيَة أَلْمَحْكِيَة لِمُتَكَلِّمي أَلإِنكِليزِيَة
The author of this book is a linguist who dissected both Arabic and English, and she simultaneously teaches both English and Arabic in two different community colleges in California. This textbook caters to the specific needs of English speakers. With the meticulous transliteration, students begin to speak Arabic from the first day of class. Arabic vowels, consonants, and nine Arabic symbols are dissected. Essential rules that govern the structure of Arabic words are discovered. No other methodology has 40+ original learning features in one program. It contains 800+ cognates. It teaches sentence patterns, grouping of words, and conjugating of verbs. As a result, students learn a methodology to teach themselves to speak indefinitely. In addition, each learned word is presented in four major Arabic dialects for the students to choose their desired dialect. It is a class-tested approach, for all ages, and it works with or without a teacher.

English Books: كُتُب بِٱلإِنكِليزِيَة لِلمؤَلِفة
1. *Read Instantly*: This book teaches English phonics to English speakers.
2. *Learn to Spell 500 Words a Day*: Each vowel is in a volume and the consonants are in a volume.
3. *100 Spelling Rules*: It contains over 100 English spelling rules discovered by the author.
4. All the Compound Words: It contains nearly all the English compound words.

About the Author: عَن ألمُوَلِفة

The author, Camilia Sadik is a linguist, and she simultaneously teaches both English and Arabic in two different community colleges in San Diego, California. She spent five long years dissecting Arabic and fifteen additional years dissecting English.

Offering Intense Courses: دِروس خِصوصِيَة لِلْطَلَبَة أو لِلْمُعَلِمين

The author Camilia Sadik or her representative offer intense workshops worldwide. The workshop may be a day or several days to teach reading and spelling in English, and to teach spoken Arabic and the Arabic Alphabet. The workshops may be for students or to train the trainers.

Visit our Arabic website: EnglishForArabicSpeakers.com
Visit our English website: SpellingRules.com
Email us: spell@spellingrules.com

Worldwide Copyright and Patents

WARNING: Copyright © by Camilia Sadik 2023. All rights are reserved. No part of this publication may be reproduced or distributed in any form or by any means. Teacher may not copy any pages or ideas from this book to distribute to students. Please note that these books are for sale at a discounted rate, whereby teachers and students each use a copy to teach or to learn.

حقوق الطبع محفوظة للمؤلفة كاميليا صادق منذ عام 2003

PART ONE
Nine Letters

Nine Letters تِسْعَة حِروف

Name	Symbol	As in	Isolated	End	Middle	Beginning
daal: دال	d	**d**ip	د	ـد	ـد	د
'elif: ألِف	aa	m**a**n	ا	ـا	ـا	ا
waaw: واو	w or oo	**w**ill or f**oo**d	و	ـو	ـو	و
raa': راء	r	**r**adio	ر	ـر	ـر	ر
zaay: زاي	z	**z**oo	ز	ـز	ـز	ز
dhaal: ذال	dh	**th**at	ذ	ـذ	ـذ	ذ
Taa': طاء	T	kilowa**tt**	ط	ـط	ـط	ط
yaa': ياء	y or ee	**y**ou or m**ee**t	ي	ـي	ـي	يـ
laam: لام	l	unti**l**	ل	ـل	ـل	لـ

➤**Note:** Don't be discouraged when you see English capital letters inside words, as in (ribaaT رباط). There aren't enough English letters to represent all the 28 Arabic letters; hence, capital English letters are used to represent a few Arabic sounds.

Chapter 1   d: د   daal: دال

The name of this Arabic letter is daal دال and it sounds like the English "d" as in dip. The symbol given in this book is "d" as in (radio: raad·yoo راديو), (Madrid: med·reed مَدْريد), and the name of the letter daal دال. The letter daal دال is a consonant. The letter daal د has two shapes, this isolated shape د and it has this cursive shape ـد to enable it to attach to 22 other letters from its right side only←. Like English cursive, 22 of the Arabic letters are connected to one another from both sides. However, these first six letters do not connect to each other, but you will see them connecting to other letters only from their right side.←

←

د   ـد

مَدْريد   دولار

Remember: Arabic is written and read from Right to Left←

Short Arabic Vowels: حَرَكات
This is a brief and early introduction of the three short Arabic vowels to enable you to read them before writing them. Do not worry about writing the short vowels yet, just read them and you will soon find the details on the short vowels in the Introduction. The three Arabic short vowels are tiny strokes or blips written above or below the consonants. Their Arabic names are called (fet'·Heh فَتْحَة, De'·meh ضَمَة, kes'·reh كَسْرَة) and they are represented by the symbols e, u, and i in this book.

(1) In this book, the English symbol for the (fetHeh فَتْحَة) is (e) and when stressed, it sounds like the English short vowel "e" as in "set." When not stressed it has a very weak sound (a schwa sound) that is barely heard as in the English final vowel in beggar, human, and bitter. This Arabic vowel is written above the consonants like this (de: دَ) whereby it is a small blip above the daal.

(2) The English symbol for the (Demeh ضَمَة) is (u) and it has a very clear and distinct sound that is just like the sound of the English "u" in "put" or in "book." The (Demeh ضَمَة) is also written above consonants like this (du: دُ) whereby the "u" sound is a small blip above the daal.

(3) In this book, the English symbol for the (kesreh كَسْرَة) is (i) and the kesreh is written <u>below</u> the consonants like this (di: دِ) whereby it is a small blip below the daal. When stressed, the kesreh sounds like the English short vowel "i" as in "sit" and like the Arabic kesreh as in (daughter/girl: bint بِنْت). However, when kesreh is not stressed, it has a weak (schwa) sound that can be confused with the sound of fetHeh as in (powder: baaw'·dir باوْدِر) and as in (one: waa'·Hid واحِد). Moreover, the kesreh at the end of a stressed word or syllable sounds like the "i" in "ski" as in (you feminine: in'in·ti إنْتِ) and as in (ri·baaT': رباط) and as in (the prefix bi: بِ in bi·doon': بدون). Note that the kesreh is stressed in common names as in Rabat: ri·baaT' رباط, Damascus: di'·mashq: دِمَشْق, and si·haam' سِهام, and the reason for that is to show formality (respect) to common names. In Egyptian dialect, the sound of kesreh whether in the middle or end of words is usually stressed.

The Arabic Alphabet for English Speakers

❶ Learning Step One: Find the د and ـد in these Arabic words and trace from right to left⟵ on top of both letter's beginning د and end ـد shapes. 🗣 Make sure that you are always uttering the sound of the letter while tracing them:

English	Transliteration	Arabic
dollar:	dōo'·laar	دولار
radio:	raad'·yoo	راديو
Sudan:	soo'·daan	سودان
Madrid:	med·reed'	مَدْريد
Trinidad:	tir·ne·daad'	تِرْنَداد
Baghdad:	begh·daad'	بَغْداد
Detroit:	dee'·trōoyt	ديترويْت
Damascus:	di'·meshq	دِمَشْق
Denmark:	de·nee'·maark	دَنيمارْك
democracy:	dee'·muq·raa·Tee·yeh	ديمُقْراطِيَة
Jordan:	'el·'ur'·dun	ألأرْدُن
doctor:	dik·tōor'	دِكْتور
doctor ♀:	dik·tōo'·reh	دِكْتورة
d:	daal:	دال
without:	bi·doon'	بِدون
I study:	'e'·na*a* 'ed'·rus	أنا أدْرُس

Part One

❷ **Learning Step Two:** Read aloud the sound of (d د) with the three short Arabic vowels above it or below and focus on the two shapes of ـد د as you read. Remember to read the sound of د and not the name of the letter daal دال. The reason for reading aloud and repeating is to enable you to quickly recognize this letter whenever you see it among 27 other Arabic letters. Read aloud many times before you begin to write any new letters. You must first read a language aloud before you begin to write it. If in a classroom, the entire class needs to read aloud slowly together in one rhythm. Read from right to left the sound of د with the three short vowels with it:

←

de: دَ

ـدَ ـدَ ـدَ ـدَ ـدَ   دَ دَ دَ دَ دَ

دَدَ دَدَ دَدَ دَدَ   دَدَ دَدَ دَدَ دَدَ

du: دُ

ـدُ ـدُ ـدُ ـدُ ـدُ   دُ دُ دُ دُ دُ

دُدَ دُدَ دُدَ دُدَ   دُدَ دُدَ دُدَ دُدَ

di: دِ

ـدِ ـدِ ـدِ ـدِ ـدِ   دِ دِ دِ دِ دِ

دِدَ دِدَ دِدَ دِدَ   دِدَ دِدَ دِدَ دِدَ

- Dots inside English transliteration words indicate a division of words into syllables.
- Italic letters in this book mean silent letters.
- A stressed syllable has a stress mark at the end of it.
- This symbol ♀ next to a word in this book means that the word is feminine in gender.
- This ō͞o means that in this case, the sound of the Arabic long vowel "**oo**" sound like the long English "**o**" as in "radiō," not like "oo" in "zoo."

4

The Arabic Alphabet for English Speakers

❸ Learning Step Three: Trace on top of the two shapes of ـد د from right to left← and make sure you are uttering the sound of "d" د each time you write it. It is this uttering that will cause you to quickly remember د whenever you see it in the future. You may begin by tracing on top of the two shapes of the letter ـد د on the first line and then practice writing it many times on the other lines provided below:

←

ـد ـد ـد ـد ـد ـد   د د د د د د

Chapter 2   aa: ا   'elif: ألف

This Arabic letter ('e'·lif ألف) is a long vowel. It sounds like the short vowel "a" as in "sat." The symbol given to the 'elif in this book is (aa) as in (radio: raad'·yōo راديو) and as in (shampoo: shaam'·boo شامبو). The long vowel 'elif is usually silent at the beginning of words as in (aa'm·ree'·kaa أمريكا), (aa'in·ki·lee'·zee إنكليزي), and as in the name of the letter (aa'e'·lif ألف). It is also silent in the beginning of syllables as in (woman: mer'·aa'eh مَرأة). The 'elif has two shapes, this isolated vertical shape ا and this cursive shape ـا is to enable it to attach itself to 22 other letters from its right side only ـا ←.

←
ا   دادا
ـا   شامْبو

❶ Learning Step One: Find, utter, and trace on top of the isolated ا and the attached shape ـا of 'elif in these Arabic words. The beginning shape of 'elif is vertical. Write this beginning shape of ا from top to bottom ↓ and then write this cursive shape ـا from right to left and then up ـا ←. See these two arrows and trace on top of ـا ا accordingly. Write all the Arabic letters from right to left ←.

ا↓   ←   ـا

radio:	raad'·yōo	راديو
Trinidad:	tir·ne·daad'	تِرْنَداد
Baghdad:	begh·daad'	بَغْداد
shampoo:	shaam'·boo	شامْبو
door:	baab	باب
Denmark:	de·nee'·maark	دَنيمارْك
Somalia:	Soo'·maal	صومال
Washington:	waa'·shin·Tin	واشِنْطِن
Taiwan:	taay'·waan	تايْوان
geography:	jugh·raaf'·yah	جُغْرافْيَة
one/someone:	waa'·Hid	واحِد
Nicaragua:	nee·kaa'·raak·weh	نيكاراكْوَة
powder:	baaw'·dir	باوْدِر
aa:	e'·lif	ألف
d:	daal	دال

The Arabic Alphabet for English Speakers

❷ **Learning Step Two:** Do not write yet, first read these sounds of ا and د together aloud. Remember to read the sound of "daa" دا and not the names of the letters daal دال or 'elif ألف . Reading aloud stores sounds in the brain subconsciously and thus no forced memorization is needed when you read aloud. You must first read a language aloud before you begin to write it. If in a classroom, the entire class needs to read aloud together. Remember to always read and write Arabic from right to left ←:

daa: دا   da: دَ   du: دُ   di: دِ

دا دا دا دا دا دا دا دا دا دا ←

داد داد داد داد داد داد داد داد داد داد

دادا دادا دادا دادا دادا دادا دادا دادا دادا دادا

داداد داداد داداد داداد داداد داداد داداد

دا داد داداد دا داد دا داد دا داد دا

دَد دِد دُد دَ دا دُ دِد دِد دَد دَد

دا دِدا دُدا دَدا دادِ دادُ دادِ دادُ دادَ

❸ **Learning Step Three:** First, trace on top of these two shapes of the letter 'elif ألف and then copy them on the next line. Make sure you are uttering the sound of the Arabic vowel "aa" as in the English word "sat" as you trace and write the ا ل :

ل ← ا↓
ل ل ل ل ل ل   ا ا ا ا ا↓
_____   _____

_____   _____

دا دا دا دا دا دا دا دا دا دا دا
_____

_____

دادا دادا دادا دادا دادا دادا دادا دادا دادا
_____

_____

Chapter 3 — oo or w: و — waaw: واو

This Arabic letter name is waaw واو and it looks like this و. Its symbol in this book is "oo" that sounds like the "oo" in "zoo". The waaw has two sounds; one is a long vowel sound and the other is a consonant sound. See the notes below to learn about its two sounds. The letter و has two shapes و ـو, isolated shape و and this cursive shape ـو is to enable it to attach itself to 22 other Arabic letters from its right side only ـو ←. See the two shapes of this letter:

←

و   وارْسو
ـو   بوت

Two sounds of the waaw: واو أَصْوات ألْحَرف

The same letter و has two sounds; one is like the long English vowel "oo" as in "zoo," and the other is like the consonant "w" as in "will." The rules to know whether the same Arabic letter و has the vowel "oo" sound or the consonant "w" sound in a word are:

1. If the letter و is at the beginning of a word, it sounds like the consonant "w" و as in: (Washington: waa·shin·Tin واشِنْطِن) and (one: waa·Hid واحِد).

2. If the letter و is at the beginning of a syllable, it also sounds like the consonant "w" و as in: (influenza: flaa·wen·zeh فْلاوَنْزَة) and (Kuwait: kuw·weyt كُوَيْت).

3. If the letter و is inside a closed syllable, it sounds like the long Arabic vowel "oo" و as in: (boot: boot بوت), (Beirut: bey·root بَيْروت), and (lemons: ley·moon لَيْمون).

4. If the letter و is at the end of a word, it will most likely sound like the vowel "oo" و as in: (shampoo: shaam·boo شامْبو) but not when it is preceded by another vowel as in the final "w" in: (waaw: واو).

5. Similarly, if the letter و is at the end of a syllable, it will most likely sound like the vowel "oo" و as in (Cuba: koo·beh كوبَة), (Sudan: soo·daan سودان), but not when it is preceded by a vowel as in: (baaw·dir باوْدِر, waaw: واو), (country: dew·leh دَوْلَة).

6. Usually, when the letter و sounds like a vowel, it sounds like the long English vowel ū as in boot: boot بوت. Occasionally, it sounds like the long English vowel ō as in (radiō: raad·yōo راديو), (music: mōo·see·qaw موسيقى), and (macaroni: meA·ka·rōo·nee مَعْكَروني). Notice that the و sounds like the long English vowel ō mainly in words derived from English and occasionally from other languages foreign to Arabic. The two Arabic words (bananas: mōoz موز) and (plums: khōokh خوخ) also have the long English ō sound as opposed to the long English ū sound, and both are derived from the Persian language. Whether the letter و is the vowel "oo" or the consonant "w." When you first see the letter و in Arabic characters, you may or may not know whether it sounds like "w" or "oo." Both "w" and "oo" are represented by the letter و in Arabic.

The Arabic Alphabet for English Speakers

❶ Learning Step One: Find, utter, and trace on top of the letter و in these Arabic words. Pay attention to both of its attached ـو ← and isolated و shapes.

1. Rule: If و is at the beginning of a word, it sounds like the consonant "w" و:

Washington:	waa'·shin·Tin	واشِنْطِن
w or oo:	waaw	واو
one/someone:	waa'·Hid	واحد
Warsaw:	waar·sōo'	وارْسو
flowers:	werd	وَرْد
flower ♀:	wer'·deh	وَرْدَة

2. Rule: If و is at the beginning of a syllable, it also sounds like the consonant "w" و:

influenza:	flaa'·win·zeh	فْلاوَنْزا
Taiwan:	taay'·waan	تايوان
Nicaragua:	nee·kaa'·raak·weh	نيكاراكْوا
microwave:	maay'·krōo·weyf	مايْكْروَيْف
Kuwait:	kuwweyt	كُوِيْت

3. Rule: If و is inside a closed syllable, it sounds like the long Arabic vowel "oo" و:

boot:	boot	بوت
Beirut:	bey'·root	بَيْروت
lemons:	ley'·moon	لَيْمون
soup:	soob	سوب
Russia:	roos'·yeh	روسْيا
Syria:	soor'·yeh	سورْيا
without:	bi·doon'	بِدون
Detroit:	dee'·trōoyt	ديتْروِيْت
Orlando:	'ōor·laan·dōo	أورْلانْدَو
bananas:	mōoz	موز
plums:	khōokh	خوخ

9

4. Rule: If the و is at the end of a word, it will most likely sound like the vowel "oo" as in "zoo." However, if a word is derived from English and contains the long ō sound, it will sound like English long ō sound:

shampoo:	shaam'·boo	شامْبو
radio:	raad'·yōo	رادْيو
Ohio:	'ōo'·haa·yōo	أوْهايو
Orlando:	'ōor·laan·dōo	أورْلاندو
Warsaw:	waar·sōo	وارْسو

5. Rule: If و is at the end of a syllable, it will most likely sound like the Arabic vowel "oo":

Cuba:	koo'·beh	كوبا
Sudan:	soo'·daan	سودان
Tunisia:	too'·nis	تونِس
Somalia:	Soo'·maal	صومال
dollar:	dōo'·laar	دولار
microwave:	maay'·krōo·weyf	مايْكْروْوِيف
oven:	'ōo'·fin	أوْفِن
Ohio:	'ōo'·haa·yōo	أوْهايو
music:	mōo'·see·qaw	موسيقى
macaroni:	meA·ke·rōo'·nee	مَعْكَروني

The Arabic Alphabet for English Speakers

❷ Learning Step Two: First read the sounds of the three learned letters ا, د, and و together and aloud. Do not write yet; you must first read a language aloud before you begin to write it. If in a classroom, the entire class needs to read aloud slowly together:

Read this و like the English vowel **oo** as in b**oo**t.

دو دو دو دا دا دود دا دادو دادا

دود دود دود دودا دودا دود دودا

دودا دودا دادو دادو داد دادا دا

داد داد دادا دادو دادو دادا دادا

داداد دوداد دادادو داداد دوداد داداد

دو دو دود دود دودا دوداد دودادو

دودادو دودود دودود دودادو دودادو دودود

دا دو دود دودا دودا دادود دادو دادودا دو

دُ دو دُ دُدُ دودُ دُود دودُ دا دَ دو دُ

دود دودَ دَدو دِدو دِدودا

Part One

🕮 Read this و like the consonant "w" as in "wit" and read aloud:

وا وا وا وا وا وا واوا واوا

وا واو واو واو واو واو واو

وا واد واد واد واد واد واد

واد وادا وادا وادا وادا وادا

داو داو داو وادوا وادوا وادوا

داوْدا داوْدا داوْدا داوا داوا داو

داوْدا داوا داو وادْوا وادا واد واوا واو وا

وِدْوُد وِد وِد وُدْوُد وُد وَدْوُد وَد وَد

ووا دِوا وُوا دُوا وَوا وِدا وُدا وَدا

The Arabic Alphabet for English Speakers

❸ **Learning Step Three:** Practice writing the beginning and end shapes و و of the letter waaw واو. Begin by tracing on top of the first line and then practice writing on the next line provided below it. Try to utter the sounds of "oo" or "w" each time you write:

←

و و و و و

ـو ـو ـو ـو ـو

دو دو دو دو دو

دا دا دا دا دا

داد دود دودا دادا دادو دادو دودا دودا

داد دودا دود واو داو داوود واو واوا

دا دو دود دودا دادو دادود دادو دادواد

13

Chapter 4		r: ر	raa': راء

This Arabic letter name is raa' راء and it sounds like the English "r" as in "rod" but with an increase in tongue rolling. The symbol given to the letter raa' راء in this book is "r" as in (radio: raad·yoo رادْيو), (Madrid: med·reed مَدْريد) and the name of the letter (raa' راء). The raa' راء is a consonant and it has two shapes, isolated shape ر and this cursive shape ـر is to enable it to attach itself to 22 other letters from its right side only←. See its two shapes again:

ر رادار ر

ـر عَرَبي

❶ Learning Step One: Utter and trace on top of the isolated ر and the attached (cursive) ـر:

r:	raa'	راء
radar:	raa'·daar	رادار
house (f):	daar	دار
houses (f):	door	دور
microwave:	maay'·krōo·we*y*f	مايْكْروْوِيف
rice:	ruzz	رُز
furnace:	fir·nis	فِرْنِس
Russia:	roos'·yeh	روسْيَة
Syria:	soor'·yeh	سورْيَة
Algeria:	'e*l*·je·zaa'·'ir	أَلْجَزائِر
macaroni:	meA·ke·roo'·nee	مَعْكَروني
camera:	kaa'·mi·reh	كامِرَة
Arizona:	'e·ree·zoo·naa	أريزونا
Rabat:	ri·baaT'	رِباط
Arabic:	Ae·re·bee'	عَرَبي
Denmark:	de·nee'·maark	دَنِمارْك
car ♀:	se*y*·yaa'·reh	سَيّارَة
school ♀:	med'·ra·seh	مَدْرَسَة

brunette ♀:	sem'·reh	سَمْرَة
Bruce:	broos	بْروس
airport:	me·Taar'	مَطار
America:	'em·ree·keh	أَمْريكا
worms:	dood	دود
dada:	daa'·daa	دادا
David:	daa'·ood	داود
medicated/healed:	daa'·waa	داوا

❷ Learning Step Two: First read the sound of "r" ر with other letters aloud many times per page and focus your eyes on the ر. Remember to read the sound of "r" ر and not the name of the letter raa' راء. If in a classroom, the entire class needs to read aloud slowly together in one rhythm. If any students can't keep up with the rhythm, ask half of the class to read first and then the other half, and keep rotating. Do not write yet; you must first read a language aloud before you begin to write it:

←

رار رار رار رار را را را را را

رور رور رور رور رو رو رو رو رو

دار دار دار دار دار دار دار دار دار

دور دور دور دور دور دور دور دور

رارا رارا رارا رارا رارا رار را

رورو رورو رورو رورو رور رور رو

راد راد راد را رود رود رو

رورا رودا رودا دارو دارو رادو رادو

رادار رادار رادا رادا دودا رورا

دور دار رور رورا دارودا دارودا دادو

🗣 Read the first و in a word or a syllable like a "w" and read aloud:

وار   وار   وار   وار   وار   وار   وارا   وارا

واد   واد   واد   واد   واد   وادا   وادا   وادا

دَوا   دَوا   رَوا   رَوا   رَوا   رَوا   رُوا   رُوا

رُوا   دُوا   دُوا   دِوا   دِوا   وِوا   وِوا

🗣 Read the و after the vowel 'elif ألف and in the beginning of a syllable like a "w":

دِوا   دِوا   رِوا   رِوا   رِوا   وِوا   وِوا

راوا   راوا   راوا   داوا   داوا   داوا   داوا

داوَر   داوَر   راوَر   راوَر   راوَر   راوَر

واوا   واوا   واوا   وارا   وارا   وارا   وار

داوا   داوا   راوا   وادا   وادا   داوَ   راوَ   واوِ

❸ **Learning Step Three**: Utter and trace on top of the two shapes of the letter raa' راء. Begin by tracing the letter on the first line and then practice copying it on the next lines provided below it:

ـر   ـر   ـر   ـر   ـر   ر   ر   ر   ر   ر

_____   _____

را   را   را   را   را   رو   رو   رو   رو   رو

_____

دار   دور   رادار   دود   دادا   داود   داوا   رو   را

_____

دار   دور   راد   رود   رورو   رارا   رورا   رور

_____

رادو   دارو   رودا   رادا   رادار   رور   دارودا   دادو

_____

داوْرو   رادار   داو   دودا   رورا   وارا

_____

16

Chapter 5

ز :z

zaay: زاي

The Arabic Alphabet for English Speakers

This Arabic letter name is zaay زاي and it sounds just like the English "z" as in "zoo". The transliteration symbol of the zaay زاي in this program is "z" as in (zebra: zee·breh زيْبْرا), (blouse: blooz بْلوز), and the name of the letter (zaay زاي). The zaay زاي is a consonant. The letter ز has two shapes, this isolated shape ز and this cursive shape ـز ← to connect it to 22 other letters from its right side only ←.

ز   زاي

ـز   إنْكِليزي

❶ Learning Step One: Read these words aloud and focus your eyes on the "zaay":

visit (v.):	zoor	زور
z:	zaay	زاي
rice:	ruzz	رُز
salad:	ze·laa'·Teh	زَلاطَة
Zaire:	zaa'·*ee*'eer	زائير
zebra:	zee'·breh	زيْبْرا
gas:	ghaaz	غاز
blouse:	blooz	بْلوز
Zeus:	zi'·yoos	زِيوس
Arizona:	'e·ree·zoo'·neh	أريزونا
Tanzania:	Ten·zaan'·yeh	طنْزانْيا
English:	'in·ki·lee'·zee	إنْكِليزي
influenza:	flaa'·win·zeh	فْلاوِنْزا
television:	te·le·fiz·yoon'	تَلَفِزْيون
Brazil:	be·raa'·zeel	بَرازيل
Venezuela:	fen·*ziwey*·leh	فَنْزَوِيلا

Part One

❷ Learning Step Two: Do not write yet, first read the sound of "z" ز with other letters aloud and focus your eyes on the two shapes of ز as you read. If in a classroom, the entire class needs to read aloud slowly together in one rhythm. If any students can't keep up with the rhythm, ask half of the class to read first and then the other half and keep rotating:

←

زا   زا   زا   زا   زا   زا   زازا   زازا   زازا

زو   زو   زو   زو   زو   زوزو   زوزو

زا   زاز   زا   زو   زوز   زوزا   زازو

زاد   زاد   زود   داز   داز   دوز   دوز

دازو   دازو   دوزو   رازو   روزا   رازا   رازا

زود   وادا   وازا   وازو   وارو   وازاد   رادو

وادو   وازار   وازور   وادوز   وازود   وادود   داوا

زاز   زَز   راز   رَز   داز   دَز   زار   زَر

واز   وَز   روز   رُز   دوز   دُز   زور   زُر

ووَد   وُد   ووز   وُز   زز   دِز   وِز   رِز

➤ The word (and: we وَ) in Arabic is not a word that can stand alone; it is the letter waaw; it's a prefix, as in (and rice: weruzz وَرُزّ). Read the prefix و in these words:

وَدار   وَدور   وَرُزّ   وَزار   وَزور   وَزاد

18

The Arabic Alphabet for English Speakers

❸ Learning Step Three: Practice writing both shapes of ز ـز in these sounds or words (phonics). Remember to stop to write the dot on the ـز before beginning to write the next letter. Also, write above the line:

ـز ـز ـز ـز   ز ز ز ز

زا زا زا زا زا زا زا زا زا زا

زو زو زو زو زو زو زو زو

راز زار زور دوز زاد داز زور راز

دازو دوزا زوزو دازا رازو روزا

زود روز زودو وادا وازا وازو وارو وازاد

وازار وازور وادوز وازود وادود

19

Chapter 6   dh: ذ   dhaal: ذال

This Arabic letter name is dhaal ذال and it sounds just like the English "th" in "that". The symbol given to the dhaal ذال in this book is "dh" as in (Heather: he·dher هَذَّر). The letter dhaal ذال is a consonant. The ذ has two shapes, this isolated shape ذ and this cursive shape ـذ is to enable it to attach to 22 other letters from its right side only. It is important to remember to place the dot right after you write the ذ before moving your pen to write the next letter. It is always necessary to complete the entire letter with all its details before beginning to write the next letter.

ذ ←
ذال
ـذ
هَذَر

❶ Find and utter this isolated ذ and this attached ـذ:

dh:	dhaal	ذال
Heather:	he′·dher	هَذَر
self-centered:	dhaa′·tee	ذاتي
this:	h<u>aa</u>·dh<u>a</u>a	هَذا
for this reason:	li·h<u>aa</u>′·dh<u>a</u>a	لِهذا
this ♀:	h<u>aa</u>′·dh<u>ee</u>h	هَذِه
Buddha:	boo′·dhaa	بوذا
Azerbeijan:	′e·dher·bey·jaan′	أَذَرْبَيجان
April:	aa·dhaar	آذار
delicious:	le·dheedh′	لَذيذ
attractive:	je·dhaab′	جَذاب
attractive ♀:	je·dhaa′·beh	جَذابة
a lie:	kidhb	كِذْب

20

The Arabic Alphabet for English Speakers

❷ Learning Step Two: First read the sound of "dh" ذ aloud with other learned letters five times per page to help you memorize all their shapes and sounds. You must first read a language aloud before you begin to write it:

←

ذاذا ذاذا ذا ذا ذاذا ذا ذا ذاذا ذاذا ذا

ذوذو ذوذو ذو ذو ذوذو ذو ذو ذوذو ذوذو ذو

ذوذ ذوذ ذوذ ذوذ ذاذ ذاذ ذاذ ذاذ ذاذ ذاذ

ذورا ذوذا ذوذا رار راد زوذ ذوز روذ

ذاز راذ ذار ذور دود ذوذ ذوذ زاذ

داذوذ زاذوذ ذاذو ذوذا ذاذا ذار زار ذار

داذوذ زاذوذ راذوذ رارو ذارا زوذا ذازا

ذاذوذ زاذا زوذو ذاذور روذا روذو راذا

واواوا ذاذاذا ذا زازازا رودانو داروذ دوذار

دادور داذور داذ ذادا ذارا ذازا ذاوا واذا

دَذاذو دَزورو ذادَذو زَروذا زورِرا واوَ وَوا

داذزوزو دُداذوذ زورِراز زاروذِذ دُذوزا

21

Part One

❸ Learning Step Three: Utter and trace on top of the two shapes of the letter dhaal ذال. Remember to write the dot on the ذ before moving your pen to write the next letter:

←

ذ ذ ذ ذ ذ   ـذ ـذ ـذ ـذ ـذ ـذ

ذا ذا ذا ذا ذا   ذو ذو ذو ذو ذو

ذوذو ذوذا ذاذو ذاد ذاذ داذ ذاذ ذوذ دود

ذوذ ذود ذود ذور ذار زار ذاذا ذوذو

ذوذا ذاذو ادو ذورا ذاذوذ دوذار راذوذ داروذ

زورار روزا دادادا رارارا زازازا ذاذاذا واواوا

22

Chapter 7 — T: ط — Taa': طاء

This Arabic letter name is Taa' طاء and it has a special sound. The closest English sound to the Arabic Taa' طاء is the "t." You will need to hear the Taa' طاء to learn it. The transliteration symbol given to the Taa' طاء in this book is a capital "T" as in the two t's in (kilowatt: kee·loo·waaT كيلوواط). Also, as in (ben·Te·loon بَنْطَلون). The Taa' طاء is a consonant that has four shapes.

➢ Similar to English cursive, the Taa' طاء and all the remaining 22 Arabic letters are connected to one another from both sides and thus have four shapes. The Taa' طاء is one of the letters that connects from both sides; it receives connections, and it gives connections as well. Its four shapes are beginning shape (connected from its left side ط), middle shape (connected from both sides ط), end shape (connected from the right side ط), and isolated shape (not connected at all ط). See the four shapes of ط in large print from right to left ←.

ط ط ط ط

طار قُطن حَط طوط

➢ Have you noticed that the four shapes of ط are actually one shape ط but they look differently because of the attachments that connect the letter to other letters? So far, you have seen the previous six Arabic letters not connecting to each other. Now, see how these same six "selfish" letters receive attachments from other letters ← and don't give such attachments to a following letter. These six letters are "selfish" because they receive attachment but don't give it:

طاطا طاطا طاطا طاطا طا طا طا طا

طوطو طوطو طو طو طو طو طو

طط طِز طِر طِذ طِد طَز طَذ طَد

ططط طَرط طَدط طُز طُذ طُد

❶ Learning Step One: Find, utter and trace on top of the beginning ط, middle ط, end ط, and isolated ط shape of ط in these Arabic words:

T:	Taa'	طاء
potatoe:	be·Taa'·Teh	بَطاطة
bottle:	bu'·Tul	بُطُل
cotton:	quTn	قُطْن
Tripoli:	Te·raa'·blus	طَرابْلُس
Rabat/necktie:	ri·baaT'	رِباط
pants:	ben·Te·loon'	بَنْطَلون
Atlanta:	'eT·laan·Te*h*	أطْلانْطا
kilowatt:	kee'·loo·waaT	كيلوْواط
restaurant:	meT'·Aem	مَطْعَم
put:	HuT	حُط
student:	Taa'·lib	طالِب
mud:	Teen	طين
toot, toot:	Toot	طوط
flew:	Taar	طار

➤ Read these so far learned letters in real words:

radar:	رادار	worms:	دود
dada:	دادا	David: daa'·ood	داود
house (f)	دار	houses (f):	دور
visit (v.):	زور	he visited:	زار
he flew:	طار	increased:	زاد
watt:	واط	toot:	طوط

🗣 Read these three sentences from right to left ←:

طوط، طوط، طوط.   طار داود.   زور داود.

The Arabic Alphabet for English Speakers

❷ Learning Step Two: First read the sound of "T" ط aloud five times per page and focus your eyes on the four shapes of Taa' طاء as you read ط ط ط ط. Remember to read the sound of T ط and not the name of the letter Taa' طاء. Not reading aloud may help you understand these sounds, but it will not help you memorize them. You must first read and speak a language aloud before you begin to write it:

طا طا طا طا طا طا طاطا طاطا

طو طو طو طو طوطو طوطو طوطو

طاط طاط طاط طاط طوط طوط طوط

طار طاد طاذ طاو طاز طاد طاطا طاط

طور طود طوذ طوز طوط طوط طوط

طا طوط طاطود طو طاط طوطاط

طاطو طوطا طارو راط داط زاط ذاط

واط روط زوط ذوط دوط ووط زوطا

روطا ذوطا دوطا زاطا راطا ذاطا واط

واطا راطا داطا ذاطو داطو دوطو ذوطو

طَطَر طُطاط زُطوط طَدار ذَطود راط روط

زاط زوط ذاط ذوط داط دوط طِوا زِطا زِروط

رِط رازِط رِطا دِطا وِطا وَطو وَطاد

رُطو رُطاد طُطا طُطاد طُطاز طُطاذ طُطار طُّطاط

طُطو طُطوط طُطود طُطا طُطاط طُطار واطِ

واطِطو طِطورا وَطِطاز راطِط ذاطِط طُّطَطِ طُّطِطِ

25

Part One

❸ Learning Step Three: Practice writing the four shapes of the letter Taa' طاء. You may need to be shown how to write this letter. It is important to remember to complete writing the ط in two steps before moving your hand to write the next letter in a word. Write the ط in two steps. Start with the bottom part of ط from right to left← and then pick up the pen to finish it from top to bottom ط ↓.

Step 1. ط ←
Step 2. ط ↓

| ططو | ط | ط | ط | | ط | ط | ط | ط | طو | ط |

| دوط | ط | ط | ط | ط | | ط | ط | ط | ططط | ط |

| ططططط | طططط | ططط | طظ | طر | طذ | طد | طو | طا |

| طود | طوط | طاد | طاذ | طاز | طاو | طار | طاط |

| روط | ذوط | زوط | دوط | طوز | طور | طود | طوذ |

| وازاط | واواطاطا | واطو | ووط | ذاط | راط | واط |

| ووط | دوط | ذوط | زوط | روط | واط | داط | ذاط | زاط |

26

❹ **Learning Step Four:** Pick the correct shape of ط ط ط ط to fill in these blanks. The Tahoma font is closer to handwritten:

ط   ط   ط   ط   ط

طار   قُطن   حَط   طوط

Handwritten
↓

ط   ط   ط   ط

←

__ا   __ا __ا   __و   __د   __ذ   __ر   __ز

__و   __و   __ا   __ار   __اور   __ود

__وذ   __از   __ا ذا   __دو   __زو   __ذو   __وا   __ا

__رو   __را   __وا   __و __ا   __واوا __ا   __وازا

__ارا   __ورا   __وا __ورا   __ادار   __ودا

__ذا __ود   __زو __ور   __زو __ذا   __رو __ا   __ادواذ

__و   __و   __و   __وا   __وا __و

__وا __و   __و __ا   __ار   __رو __ا   __ذو

__ارو   __ا __ا   __رو   __زا __ا   __از   __را __و

__زورو   __راوزا   __دارو   __ذاوا __ا   __ادار

__ودا   __ذا __ود   __زو __ور   __زو __ذا   __ادواذ

__رو __ا __ا   __ط__ار   __ط َط__ِ   __ط__ُ   __واطِ __و

__ط__ا   __ط__ا   __ط__از   __ط__ار   __ط __اط

27

Chapter 8 — y or ee: ي — yaa': ياء

This Arabic letter name is yaa' ياء and its symbol in this book is "ee" that sounds like the "ee" in "meet". The yaa' has two sounds; one is a long vowel sound and the other is a consonant sound. See the notes below to learn its two sounds. The yaa' has four shapes beginning ـيـ, middle ـيـ, end ـي, and isolated ي. Do not write before reading. First, see these four shapes of the letter yaa' ياء alone and in words ←:

The yaa' sounds: أَصوات أَلْياء

The same letter yaa': ياء has two sounds, one is a long vowel sound that sound like the long English vowel "ē" as in zēbra and as in lucky, and the other is a consonant sound like the English "y" as in "yes." In this book, the symbols "ee" as in (cinema: see·ne·maa سينَما) is given to the vowel sound of yaa' and the symbol "y" as in (yoo·ghis·laaf·yeh يوغِسلافْيا) is given to the consonant sound of the yaa' ياء. The rules to know whether the same Arabic letter ـيـ ـيـ ـي ي in its four shapes has the long vowel "ē" sound or the consonant "y" sound in a word are:

1. If the letter ـيـ is at the beginning of a word ـيـ it sounds like the consonant "y" ـيـ as in: (yahoo: yaa·hoo ياهو), (Yolanda: yoo·laan·dah يولاندا), (Yugoslavia: yoo·ghis·laaf·yaa يوغِسلافْيا), (Uganda: yoo·ghen·deh يوغَنْدة), and (yaa': ياء).

2. If the letter ـيـ is at the beginning of a syllable, it also sounds like the consonant "y" as in (radio: raad·yoo راديو), (geography: jugh·raaf·yeh جُغْرافْيَة), (Russia: roos·yaa روسْيا), and (Syria: soor·yeh سوريَة).

3. If the letter ـيـ is inside a closed syllable, it sounds like the long vowel "ee" ي as in (Brazil: be·raa·zeel بَرازيل), (Palestine: fe·les·Teen فَلَسْطين), (delicious: le·dheedh لَذيذ), and (milk: He·leeb حَليب).

4. If the letter ي is at the end of a word, it will most likely sound like the vowel "ee" ي as in (Malaysia: maa·lee مالي), (jell-O: je·lee جَلي), (macaroni: meA·ke·roo·nee مَعْكَروني), (Arabic: Ae·re·bee عَرَبي), (English: 'in·ki·lee·zee إنْكِليزي), unless the yaa' is preceded by a vowel as in (house: beyt بَيت), (lemons: ley·moon لَيْمون), (zaay زاي), and (Taiwan: taay·waan تايْوان).

5. Similarly, if the letter ي is at the end of a syllable, it will most likely sound like the vowel "ee" ي as in (Lena: lee·neh لينا), (zebra: zee·braa زيبْرا), (cinema: see·ne·maa سينَما), and American: ('em·ree·kee أَمْريكي).

The Arabic Alphabet for English Speakers

➤ See how these first six Arabic letters (ا و د ذ ر ز) connect to other letters only from their left side ← but they stop giving connections to letters on their right side:

ياذ   يوذ   يِدِز   يُذْط   يَرد   يُري

طاطا   طوط   طِدو   طُذا   طَري   طُزو

❶ Learning Step One: Find, utter, and trace on top of the isolated and the attached (cursive) shapes of the yaa' ي in these Arabic words. Remember that unless the final yaa' is preceded by a vowel, it will be "**ee**" not "y" as in:

Malaysia:	maa'·lee	مالي
jell-O:	je·lee'	جَلي
macaroni:	meA·ke·roo'·nee	مَعْكَروني
Arabic:	Ae'·re·bee	عَرَبي
English:	'in·ki·lee'·zee	إنْكْليزي
my home:	daa'·ree	داري
American:	'em·ree'·kee	أمْريكي
Lena:	lee'·neh	لينَه
cinema:	see'·ne·maa	سينَما
America:	'em·ree'·kaa	أمْريكا
zebra:	zee'·braa	زيْرا
my book:	k*i*taa'·bee	كِتابي
my mother:	'u'·mee	أمي
low:	waa'·Tee	واطي

➤ If the letter yaa' is inside a closed syllable, it is "ee" not "y" as in:

Brazil:	be·raa'·zeel	بَرازيل
delicious:	le·dheedh'	لَذيذ
Palestine:	fe·lis·Teen'	فَلَسْطين

fly (v.):	Teer	طير
milk:	He·leeb'	حَليب
Zaire:	zaa'·*ee*'eer	زائير

➤The ‍ي at the beginning of a word or a syllable ‍ي sounds like the consonant "y" as in:

y or ee:	yaa'	ياء
yahoo:	yaa'·hoo	ياهو
Yolanda:	yoo'·laan·deh	يولانْدا
Uganda:	yoo'·ghaan·deh	يوغانْدة
Yugoslavia:	yoo'·ghis·laaf'·yeh	يوغِسْلافْيا
radio:	raad'·yoo	رادْيو
geography:	jugh·raaf'·yeh	جُغْرافْية
Russia:	roos'·yeh	روسْيا
Syria:	soor'·yeh	سورْيَة

➤The yaa' after a vowel sounds like "y" as in:

house:	be*y*t	بَيت
lemons:	ley·moon'	لَيْمون
Taiwan:	taay'·waan	تايْوان
z:	zaay:	زاي
days:	'e·yaam'	أيّام

The Arabic Alphabet for English Speakers

❷ Learning Step Two: First read the two sounds of يـ ـيـ ـي ي aloud five times per page and focus on the four shapes of yaa' ياء. Not reading aloud may help you understand these sounds, but it will not help you remember them. Do not write yet; you must first read a language aloud before you begin to write it:

يا يايا يايا يايا يو يو يويو يويو يي

يي يييي يييي يايا يويو يايا يايا طايا

وايا ذايا طويا طويو دويو رايو طيد طيذ

طير طيط طيطير واطي طي راطي زاطي ذاطي

داطي طاطي ياطي طازي رازي زازي يازي

وازي زاري وادي دادي داري دي ذي زي

ري وي طي ويزي طيطي ريري طيطا يور يود

يوط يوذي زادي ذيذي زيزي ويزي ديدي طيطاوي

طيراز دُرْزي وَطيد طير طَيْر طَيْري دَيْر

دَيْري يَد يَدي دار داري دور دوري وَ دار

وَدار وَداري وَ وَرازي وَزيري وَديدي وَزير

وَوَزير يُداري يَدْري يَذْوي يَطير يَطْوي

طِط طَط طُط طِط طُط يُط يَط

31

Part One

❶ Read the ياء that is preceded by a vowel like a "y" as in (house: be*y*t بَيْت), (lemons: ley·moon لَيْمون), zaay (زاي), (Taiwan: taay·waan تايْوان), and these examples:

داي زاي ذاي ياي طاي واي واىواي دَي زَي

رَي ذَي طَي يَي وَي زَي زُي رُي دُي وُي

يُي طُي دُي دُيْدي

❸ Learning Step Three: Practice writing the four shapes of the yaa'. Remember to finish writing the entire letter before beginning to write the next letter. Begin by writing the top of the letter and immediately after that add the two dots below it:

ي يـ يـ ي ي

ي يـ يـ ي ي

طيا ـيـ ـيـ ـيـ ـيـ يـ يـ يـ يا

طي ي ي ي ي ـي ـي ـي

ذايا وايا يايا يز يذ يد يو يا

طير طيد رايو دويو طويو طويا طايا

زادي داطير طي طيي طيذ طيد

ياطو طيطا طيطو طيطو ريري زيزي ذيذي

طيطاوي   طيطي   ذيط   واطي   راي   دوي   ذي

_____

ذوذي   طازي   رازي   بيي   بيبي   بيطي

_____

داي   زاي   راي   ذاي   طاي   ياي   واي   وايواي

_____

❹ Pick the correct shape of ي to fill in these blanks:

ي   ـي   ـيـ   يـ
ي   ـي   ـيـ   يـ

__ا __ا __ا __و __و __و __د __ر __ر __ز

داط __ر   زاد __ ذ   ذ __ ز __ ز __ و __ ر __ ر

و __ ز __ طاط __ ط __ طو ط __ طا __ طو

ط __ طاو __ را __ دو __ ذوذ __ طاز __ راز

ط __ ط __ واز __ ذ __ ط __ واط __ ط __ راز

طازوط __ طط __ ذ __ وط __ د __ طط __ ذ __ طط __ ر

طط __ ط __ ط __ د __ ط __ ر __ ط __ طذ __ ط __ ز

طط __ ط __ ط __ د __ ط __ ر __ ط __ ز __ ط __ ر

داط __ زاط __ واط __ ط __ زاز __ طاز __ طاط __

__ اط __ وط __ د __ ياز __ زار

Extra Practice

📢 Read these so far learned letters in these real words:

raadaar:	رادار	dood:	دود
daadaa:	دادا	daa'·ood:	داود
daar:	دار	door:	دور
waaT:	واط	TooT:	طوط
raadyō:	رادْيو	zaay:	زاي
waadee:	وادي	rey:	رَي
dee'·dee:	ديدي	zee'·zee:	زيزي
raa'·zee:	رازي	zeyd:	زَيْد
durz:	دُرز	dur·zee:	دُرزي
Teyr:	طَير	Teyree:	طَيري
yed:	يَد	yedee:	يدي
deyr:	دَير	deyree:	دَيري
werd:	وَرد	wezeer	وزير
zey:	زَي	zeyee:	زَيي
waaTee:	واطي	werdee:	وَرْدي

Past tense masculine verbs:

he visited:	زار	he/it became more:	زادَ
he flew:	طار	he medicated/healed:	داوا
he took care of:	دارا	he made parallel:	وازا

Command form masculine verbs:

visit:	زور	become more:	زيد
fly:	طير	medicated/heal:	داوي
care for:	داري	make parallel:	وازي
and:	وَ		

The Arabic Alphabet for English Speakers

➢ The English word "and" is a prefix in Arabic it consists of the letter waaw+fetHeh وَ. It sounds like we: وَ in FuSHaw فُصْحى, like wi: و in Egyptian dialect and like w: و without the vowel above it, because the vowel is silent in certain dialects. Read aloud and see how the prefix و precedes nouns, verbs, and adjectives in these examples:

The و before nouns:

and Raazee:	weraa'·zee	ورازي
and Deedee:	wedee'·dee	وديدي
and Zeezee:	wezee'·zee	وزيزي
and David:	wedaa'·ood	وداود
and zayd:	wezeyd	وزَيْد
and a radio:	weraad'·yoo	وراديو
and a radar:	weraa'·daar	ورادار
and worms:	wedood	ودود
and a zaay:	wezaay	وزاي
and Ray:	werey	ورَي
and a minister:	wi·we·zeer'	ووَزير
and a valley:	wi·waa'·dee	ووادي
and flowers:	wi·werd'	ووَرد
and my flowers:	wi·wer·dee'	ووَرْدي
and a bird:	weTeyr	وطَير
and my bird:	weTey·ree'	وطَيري
and a hand:	weyed	ويَد
and my hand:	weye·dee'	ويَدي
and an abbey:	wedeyr	ودَير
and my abbey:	wedey·ree'	ودَيري

The و before adjectives and before Egyptian words (like or as: زَي):

and pink:	wewer·dee'	ووَرْدي

35

and Durz:	wedur·zee′	دُرْزي
and low:	wi·waa′·Tee	وِواطي
and like (Egyptian):	wi·zey′	وِازي
and like me (Egyptian):	wi·ze·yee′	وِزَيِي

The "e" is silent in "we" except in (he made parallel: وَوازا):

and he visited:	وَزار	and it increased:	وَزاد
and he flew:	وَطار	and he medicated:	وَداوا
and he cared for:	وَدارا		

The و before command form verbs:

and medicate:	wedaa′·wee	وَداوي
and fly:	weTeer	وَطير
and care for:	wedaa′·ree	وَداري

ye: يَ

The prefixes ye: يَ conjugate a verb from a command form verb, as in (fly (v.): Teer طير) to a masculine present tense verb, as in (he flies: yeTeer يَطير) and as in (care for: daa·ree يُداري). The sound of the vowel "e" in "ye" varies in different dialects. See these examples:

he flies:	yeTeer	يَطير
he folds:	yi·Twee′	بِطوي
he hallucinates:	yi·dhwee′	بِذوي
he takes care of:	yudaa′·ree	يُداري
he medicates/heals:	yudaa′·wee	يُداوي
he knows:	yid·ree′	بِدري

yaa: يا

The yaa: يا is an optional calling word placed before a person's name, title, or description, as in (hey you Raazee: yaa raa·zee: يا رازي). Literally translated, the yaa: يا means "a calling device". The closest translation of the yaa: يا to English would be, for instance, "hey you John", but with much more respect than in the English "hey you".

←

يا رازي!   يا داود!   يا ديدي!   يا زيزي!   يا وَزير!   يا وَرْد!   يا طَير.

🗣Read these phrases and sentences aloud many times and read them mainly for the sake of learning the alphabet, not for the sake of learning every grammatical detail:

←

داري رازي.   داوي ديدي.   زور داود.   داوي داود.   زور داود

يا رازي.   وَداوي زَيد يا رازي.   وَداري زيزي.   رازي زار داود.

رازي داوا زَيد.   رازي دارا زيزي.   رازي زار داود وَزار ديدي.

رازي زار داود وَديدي وَزيزي.   رازي يَطير   رازي يداري ديدي.

يُداوي زَيد.   رازي يداري زيزي وَديدي.   رازي

يداري زيزي وَيداري ديدي.   رازي دُرزي.   رازي وَزير.

رازي وَرد.   رازيي زَيي.   يَدي زَيي يَد رازي.   طَيري زَي طَير

رازي.   طَيري يَطير.   طَيري يطير يا زيزي.   طَيري

طار.   طَيري طار يا زيزي.   طَيري يطير واطي.   طَير يا طَير.

طَير يا طَيري.   طوط، طوط، طوط.

➤These are phrases of Arabic nouns preceding adjectives:

وادي واطي   راديو واطي   وَرد وَرْدي   طَير وَرْدي

37

Chapter 9   l: ل   laam: لام

This Arabic letter name is laam لام and it has a light sound of "l" like the English "l" in "until". The letter laam لام is a consonant and it is given the symbol "l" in this book as in (kilo: kee·lōo·كيلو), (pants: ben·Te·loon بَنْطَلون), and (bottle: bu·Tul بُطُل). Like the rest of the remaining Arabic letters, the laam لام has four shapes: beginning لـ, middle ـلـ, end ـل, and isolated ل. Do not write yet; first see the four shapes of laam لام from right to left:

←

لـ   ـلـ   ـل   ل

لَيْمون   بْلوز   بَرازيل   دال

❶ Learning Step One: Find, trace, and utter the four shapes of laam: لام in these Arabic words:

d:	daal	دال
dh:	dhaal	ذال
aa:	'e'·lif	أَلِف
blouse:	blooz	بْلوز
bottle:	bu'·Tul	بُطُل
delicious:	le·dheedh'	لَذيذ
lemons:	ley·moon'	لَيْمون
Somalia:	'el·Soo'·maal	ألصومال
English:	'in·ki·lee'·zee	إنْكِليزي
Brazil:	be·raa'·zeel	بَرازيل
television:	te·le·fiz·yōon'	تَلَفِزيون
Algeria:	'el·je·zaa'·'ir	ألْجَزائِر
Istanbul:	'is·Ten·bool'	إسْطَنْبول
Tripoli:	Te·raa'·blus	طَرابْلُس
guide (n.):	de·leel'	دَليل
student:	Taa'·lib	طالِب
pants:	ben·Te·loon'	بَنْطَلون
toilet:	tawaa'·ley*t*	تِوالَيْت

lamp ♀	lem'·beh	لَمْبَة
jell-O:	je·lee'	جَلي
penicillin:	ben·se·leen'	بَنْسَلين
alcohol:	ki·Hool'	كِحول
Libya ♀:	leeb'·yaa	ليبْيا
London:	len'·den	لَنْدَن
Malaysia:	maa'·lee	مالي
Palestine:	fe·les·Teen'	فَلَسْطين
Malta ♀:	maal'·Taa	مالْطا
film:	film	فِلْم
millionaire:	mil·yōo'·ney·yer	مِلْيونَير
Lena ♀:	lee'·naa	لينا
Linda ♀:	lin'·daa	لِندا
the:	'el	أَلْـ
food:	'ekl	أَكْل

➢ Punctuations in Arabic:

period: .   comma: ،
exclamation mark: !   question mark: ؟
colon: :   semicolon: ؛
A period also means the number zero: .

Part One

❷ Learning Step Two: Read the laam ل with other learned letters and read aloud five times per page. If you repeat and read aloud, you will quickly retain what you learn. Do not write yet; you must first read a language aloud before you begin to write it:

←

لي   ليلي   ليلي   لي   لي   لولو   لو   لو   لو

ذال   دال   ليل   ليل   ليل   ليل   ليلو   ليلو

زول   رول   ذول   دول   يال   طال   وال   زال   رال

ذيل   زيل   ريل   ديل   طيل   ليل   يول   طول   وول

ذيلي   زيلي   ريلي   ليلي   طيلي   ليلو   طيل   ويل

طاولي   ليالي   دَوالي   لوري   والي   وادي   ديلي   ويلي

لَيل   وَلَد   رَذاذ   يَطول   يَلِد   يَلْوي   يَزور   يَريد

لِليل   لِلي   لِرازي   لِلوَلَد   دَليل   ريال   زَوال   ذَيل

طال   يُطارِد   يُطيل   طَويل   طول   لَذيذ   لَدود   وَزير

طَل   زال   وليد   ديلور   دَليلي   طاليا   داليا   زاد   دَليل

ديدي   ريدي   دَي   رَي   ذَل   رَزيل   زوزي   دَيْزي

يُلَطْلِط   دَوْلي   دُول   زَي   زاوَل   وارِد   وَريدي   وَرْدي

لَلوالي   لُلِلي   لَلول   لُلَل   لَيْل   لِذا   لَطْلِط   يُليط

40

The Arabic Alphabet for English Speakers

➤ Note: Do not confuse the shapes of the middle laam that looks like this ⊥ with that of the end 'elif that looks like this ㄴ. Remember that the final 'elif ㄴ is selfish because it receives connection from a preceding letter but does not give connection to a following letter ㄴ whereas the middle ⊥ is connected from both sides. Practice writing the two letters to remember their differences:

⊥ ⊥ ⊥ ⊥ ⊥   ㄴ ㄴ ㄴ ㄴ ㄴ ㄴ

طلط   يلط   يَلي   طِلي   طـا   طـار   يا   يار

❸ Learning Step Three: Practice writing these four shapes of the letter laam لام:

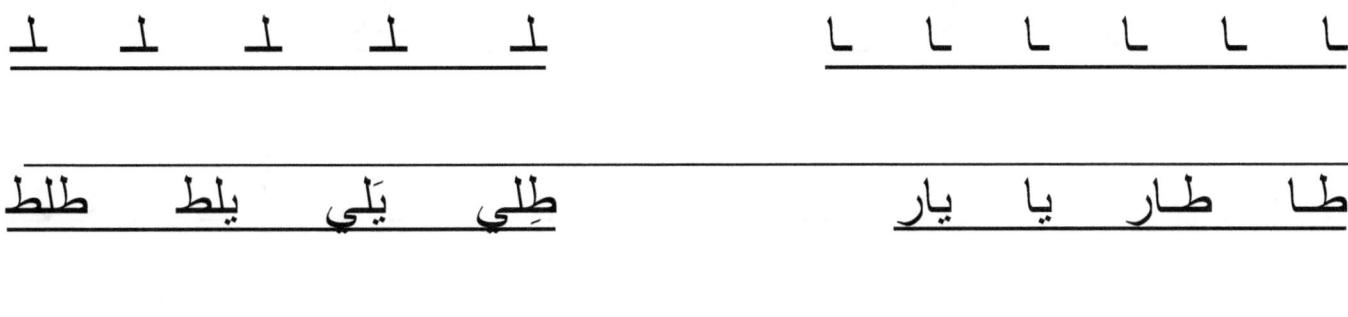

⊥ ⊥ ⊥ ⊥ ⊥   ـل ـل ـل ـل ـل

ل ل ل ل ل ل   ـلـ ـلـ ـلـ ـلـ ـلـ

لدا   لزا   لرا   لِذا   لَيل   ليلو   لي   لولو   لو

دل   ديلي   ويلي   ذيلي   زيلي   ريلي   ليلي   طيلي

ليلو   طويل   طيل   ويل   ذيل   زيل   ريل   ديل

زال ذال دال يول طول وول زول رول ذول

والي دول يال طال ليل يطلي يلي طلي

لللطللل ليالي طاولي ليليطليلول لوري

❹ Pick the correct shape of the letter laam لام to fill in these blanks:

ل   لـ   ـلـ   ـل

ل   لـ   ـلـ   ـل

←

__و   لو__و   لي__و   لي__   __ذا   د__   طي__ي

دي__   زي__   ذي__   وي__   طي__   طوي__   __يلو

ذو__   رو__   زو__   طو__   يو__   دا__   ذا__

__يلي   زي__ي   طلا__   __ي__ط__ط   __و__   د__

دي__   __ذا   ذيذ__   __يطا__ي   __وري   ريا__

دا__يا   طا__يا   راي__   __يا__ي   طاو__ي   __يلول

__ذا   __ولد   لولد__   __رازي   __لي   __ل__يل

__ي__و   ط__يل   طا__يل   __يلط__   طوي__

l+aa: لا

The laam لام followed by an 'elif ألف sounds like laa but the combination of the two letters is not written like this لا. Instead, laa is written like this لا or when attached like this ﻼ. In print, the beginning shape of laa: لا looks like this لا as in (Orlando: 'ōr·laan·dō أورلاندو). The middle or end shape of laa: لا looks like this ﻼ as in (plastic: blaa·steek بلاستيك). Whether in the beginning, middle or end, handwritten laa: لا look like this لا. See the shapes below. Imagine the 'elif hopping into the lap of the laam لام like the way a baby kangaroo hops into its mother's belly:

$$\overleftarrow{ﻟ+ﺎ} = لا \text{ or } ﻼ$$

Not this → لا

Handwritten لا لا

> The laa لا has an isolated shape لا and an attached from its right side shape ﻼ. Trace both shapes of laa in these Arabic words. Make sure that you are uttering the sound of the letters while tracing them:

l:	laam	لام
Las Vegas:	laas fey·kes	لاس فيْكَس
no:	laa	لا
must:	laa·zim	لازِم
Orlando:	'ōr'·laan·dōo	أورْلانْدو
salad ♀:	ze'·laa·Teh	زَلاطَة
Jordan:	'el·aa'ur'·dun	الأرْدُن
Alaska ♀:	'e·laa'·skaa	ألاسْكا
influenza ♀:	flaa'·win·zaa	فْلاوَنْزا
Atlanta ♀:	'eT·laan'·Taa	أطْلانتا
classical:	klaa'·see·kee	كْلاسيكي
plastic:	blaa'·steek	بْلاسْتيك
glass:	klaaS	كْلاص
Oklahoma ♀:	'ōok·laa·hōo·maa	أوكْلاهوما
peace:	se·laam'	سَلام
goodbye:	me'·Ae 'el·se·laa'·meh	مَعَ ألسَلامَة
English ♀:	'elaa'in·ki·lee'·zi·yeh	إنْكِليزي

Part One

🔊 Read the following sounds aloud many times:

لا لا لا لا لا لا لا لا لا لا لا لا لا

طَلال رولاد وِلاد لاد لاذ لاز لاي لاط

لاوزي زُلا وَلا لاري دولار زَلاط دِلايلا

لَلا وَلا لولا طَلا لالي ويلا ديلا طيلا

➤ The handwritten laa لا looks different. Practice writing the laa from right to left:

لا لا لا لا لا   لا لا لا لا لا

ويلا للا لاط لاي لاز لار لاذ لاد ولاد

ديلايلا طلا رولادو طَلال وَلا طيلا ديلا

Handwritten ↓
This Tahoma font sort of resembles handwritten Arabic letters.

لا لا لا لا لا   لا لا لا لا لا

لار لاذ لاد وِلاد للا لاط لاي لاز

طلا رولادو طَلال وَلا

44

The Arabic Alphabet for English Speakers

Extra Practice

👁‍🗨 Read these words that contain the so far learned letters and focus more on the alphabet and less on the grammar:

d:	daal	دال
dh:	dhal	ذال
don't/doesn't:	maa	ما
mist:	re·dhaadh'	رَذاذ
Saudi currency:	ri·yaal'	رِيال
common male name:	we·leed'	وَليد
common male name:	dee'·loor	ديلور
Larry	ley·ree'	لَيْري

➤ The word "night" and other words derived from it are sung in an enormous number of Arabic love songs:

night:	leyl	لَيل
my night:	ley·lee'	لَيْلي
nights:	le·yaa'·lee	لَيالي
for a night:	li·leyl'	لِلَيل
for the night:	lil·leyl'	لِلَّيل

The Prefix li-: لِ

This prefix means "for" or "belongs to" as in لرازي or it may mean "until" as in (until night لِلَّيل).

for raazee:	li·raa'·zee	لِرازي
belongs to raazee:	li·raa'·zee	لِرازي
for me/belongs to me:	lee'	لي
for the one that:	lil·lee'	لِلي
belongs to the one that:	lil·lee'	لِلي
for this reason:	li·dhaa'	لِذا
for /belongs to the boy	li'·we·led	لِلوَلَد

45

Possessives:

boy/son:	we'·led	وَليد
my boy/my son:	we·le·dee'	وَليدي
guide:	de·leel'	دَليل
my guide:	de·lee'·lee	دَليلي
night:	le*y*l	لَيل
my night:	le*y*·lee'	لَيلي
tail:	dheyl	ذَيْل
vein:	we'·reed	وَريد
my vein:	we·ree'·dee	وَريدي
backgammon:	Taaw'·lee	طاوْلي
ruler (male):	waa'·lee	والي
mine:	maa'·lee	مالي
big truck:	loo'·ree	لوري
my truck:	looree maalee	لوري مالي

Adjectives, nouns, verbs, etc.:

delicious:	le·dheedh'	لَذيذ
tightwad:	re·zeel'	رَزيل
income:	waa'·rid	وارد
mortified:	dhe·leel'	ذَليل
humiliated (v.):	dhil	ذَل
countries:	di'·wel	دِوَل
national/ of countries:	di·we·lee'	دِوَلي
tall:	Te·weel'	طَويل
length (n.):	Tool	طول
the entire (time):	Teel	طِيل

46

became lengthy:	Taal	طَال
becoming lengthy:	ye·Tool'	يَطول
makes matter long:	yu·Teel'	يُطيل
he wants:	yereed	يَريد
he visits:	yezoor	يَزور
it goes away:	yezool	يَزول
he twists:	yil·wee'	يَلْوي
he chases:	yuTaa'·rid	يُطارِد
it becomes born:	ye'·lid	يَلِد
worked as:	zaa'·wel	زاوَل
Daisy ♀:	dey·zee'	ديزي
Female name:	zee'·zee	زيزي
wish/want (v.) ♀:	ree'·dee	ريدي
no:	laa	لا
and not:	welaa	وَلا
if:	le·oo'	لَوْ
if not:	le·oo'·laa	لَوْلا
dollar	doo'·laar	دولار
egg white:	zu·laal'	زُلال
boys/sons (e):	wi·laad'	وِلاد
male name:	Te·laal'	طَلال

Bravo! You have Learned Nine out of 28 Arabic Letters!

The Nine Learned Letters تِسْعَة حِروف

Name	Symbol	As in	Isolated	End	Middle	Beginning
daal: دال	d	**d**ip	د	ـد	ـد	د
'elif: أَلِف	aa	m**a**n	ا	ـا	ـا	ا
waaw: واو	w or oo	**w**ill or f**oo**d	و	ـو	ـو	و
raa': راء	r	**r**adio	ر	ـر	ـر	ر
zaay: زاي	z	**z**oo	ز	ـز	ـز	ز
dhaal: ذال	dh	**th**at	ذ	ـذ	ـذ	ذ
Taa': طاء	T	kilowa**tt**	ط	ـط	ـط	ط
yaa': ياء	y or ee	**y**ou or m**ee**t	ي	ـي	ـي	ي
laam: لام	l	unti**l**	ل	ـل	ـل	ل

PART TWO

Nine Symbols that are Not Letters تِسْع حَرَكات وَرموز

All of the following nine characters that you will be studying until the end of Part Two in this book are not considered letters. The three short Arabic vowels are called fetHeh فَتْحَة, Demeh ضَمَة, and kesreh كَسْرَة and they are tiny strokes or blips written above or below the consonants. The names of these nine symbols are:

1. fet'·Heh فَتْحَة (above consonants)
2. De'·meh ضَمَة (above consonants)
3. kes'·reh كَسْرَة (<u>below</u> consonants)
4. si·koon' سِكون (above consonants)
5. shed'·deh شَدَّة (above consonants)
6. med'·deh مَدَة (above 'elif only)
7. 'e'·lif meq·Soo'·reh ألف مَقصورة (at end of words only)
8. ten·ween' تَنْوين (above and below letters)
9. hem'·zeh هَمْزَة. (alone or riding on long vowels)

Name of Symbol	As in	English Symbol	Arabic Symbol
fetHeh: فَتْحَة	s**e**t or hum**a**n	e	as in: d**e** دَ
Demeh: ضَمَة	p**u**t or w**oo**d	u	as in: d**u** دُ
kesreh: كَسْرَة	s**i**t or sk**i**	i	as in: d**i** دِ
sikoon: سِكون	**bl** in **bl**end	no vowel	as in: **d** دْ
sheddeh: شَدَّة	la**dd**er	double letters	as in: **dd** دَّ
meddeh: مَدَة	**Al**: آل	ă	as in: آل
'elif meqSooreh: ألف مَقصورة	l**aw**	aw: ley**law**	as in: لَيْلى
tenween: تَنْوين	Lond**on**: lend**en**	end **an, un, in**	كِتاباً، كِتابٌ، كِتابٍ
hemzeh: هَمْزَة	'Uh 'Oh: 'oo 'oo	'	داء، أب، إلى، زائير، قارِيء، لؤلؤ

Chapter 1: kesreh كَسْرَة	Demeh ضَمَّة	fetHeh فَتْحَة

Short Vowels حَرَكات دِ دُ دَ

(1) fetHeh فَتْحَة as in (de: دَ):
This book's English symbol for the fet'·Heh فَتْحَة is (e) and when stressed the fetHeh فَتْحَة sounds like the short English "e" as in "set." When not stressed, it has a very weak sound (a schwa sound) that is barely heard as in the final English "e" in "letter" or like the "a" in "human." This Arabic vowel is written above the consonants like this de: دَ whereby e: is a small blip above the daal: دَ. The fetHeh فَتْحَة is the shorter version of the long Arabic vowel ('elif: aa). Read the fetHeh فَتْحَة written above these consonants:

دَ   دَدَ   دَوالي   رادَ   يَريد   طَلا   وَوَرْد

(2) Demeh ضَمَّة as in (du: دُ):
This book's English symbol for the De'·meh ضَمَّة is (u) and it has a very clear and distinct sound that is just like the sound of the English "u" in "put" or the "oo" in "book." The Demeh ضَمَّة is also written above consonants like this du: دُ whereby the u: is a small blip above the consonant daal: دُ. The Demeh ضَمَّة is the shorter version of the long Arabic vowel waaw واو, and it looks like a tiny version of it. Read the Demeh ضَمَّة as it is written above these consonants:

دُ   دُدُ   دُرزي   زُلال   يُداري   يُطيل

(3) kesreh كَسْرَة as in (di: دِ):
The English symbol for the kes'·reh كَسْرَة in this book is (i) and the kesreh كَسْرَة is written <u>below</u> the consonants like this di: دِ whereby the i: دِ is a small blip below the daal: دِ. When stressed, the kesreh كَسْرَة sounds like the English "i" as in "sit" and the Arabic "i" as in (daughter/girl: bint بِنْت). However, kesreh كَسْرَة is usually not stressed and its weak (schwa) sound can be confused with the sound of fetHeh فَتْحَة as in (powder: baaw'·dir باودِر) and as in (one: waa'·Hid واحِد). Moreover, the kesreh كَسْرَة at the end of stressed words or syllables sounds like the "i" in "ski" as in the Arabic words (you ♀: 'in·ti إنْتِ) and as in the Arabic prefix bi: بِ as in (without: bi·doon': بِدون), and as in (ri·baaT': رباط). Note that the kesreh كَسْرَة is stressed in common names as in (Rabat: ri·baaT' رباط), (Damascus: di'·meshq: دِمَشْق), and (si·haam' سِهام). The reason for that is to show formality (respect) to the common names. Also, the sound of kesreh كَسْرَة whether in the middle or end of words is usually stresses in Egyptian dialect. The kesreh كَسْرَة is the shorter version of the long Arabic vowel ee: ي as in "zeezee". Read the kesreh written <u>below</u> these consonants in two different fonts; the second font is closest we can find for a handwritten font:

دِ   وادِد   وارِد   وِلاد   لِرازي   لِذا

دِ   وادِد   وارِد   وِلاد   لِرازي   لِذا

The Arabic Alphabet for English Speakers

Practice reading and then writing the short vowels above or below these consonants:

دَ دَدَ دَوالي رادَ يَريد طَلا وَوْرْد

دُ دُدُ دُرزي زُلال يُداري يُطيل

دِ وادِد وارد وِلاد لِرازي لِذا

دِ دِ وادِد وارد وِلاد لِرازي لِذا

دَ دُ دُ دِ دِ دُرْز لَو وَرْد يَد لِلي

دَوالي وَوَرَد دُرْزي يُطيل لِرازي وارد وادِد

| Chapter 2 | meddeh مَدَّة | sheddeh شَدَّة | sikoon سكون |

The Arabic Alphabet for English Speakers

آ ٱ دَّ دَّ دْ

(1) sikoon سِكون دْ as in (food: 'ekl أكْل):
The word si·koon' سكون literally means "no sound." The sikoon سِكون is a tiny circle written above a letter to assert the no vowel existence, as in the sikoon سكون above the "d" in (he knows: yid·ree' يدْري). When there is no vowel between two consonants, there can be a sikoon سكون. Sometimes, a sikoon can be at the end of words too, as in (mother: 'um أمْ). What English calls a consonant blend; Arabic calls a sikoon سِكون. Find the sikoon سكون mainly between two consonant and then trace on top of it:

دْ

Orlando:	'ōor·laan'·dōo	أورْلانْدو
food:	'ekl	أكْل
meat:	leHm	لَحْم
bread:	khubz	خُبْز
penicillin:	ben·se·leen'	بَنْسَلين
Libya:	leeb'·yaa	ليبْيا
London:	len'·den	لنْدَن
Palestine:	fe·les·Teen'	فَلَسْطين
mother:	'um	أمْ
eat (command form):	kul	كُلْ
the:	'el	أَلْ
for the/ to the/till the:	lil	لِلْ
for or till the night:	lil·leyl'	لِلْلَيل
for/ belongs to the one that:	lil·lee'	لِلْلي

🕮Practice writing the sikoon سكون above these learned consonants:

دْ   ذْ   رْ   زْ   وْ   كْ   يْ   طْ   أَلْ   لِلْلَيْل   لِلْلي

The Arabic Alphabet for English Speakers

(2) sheddeh شَدَّة as in (rice: ruzz رُزّ):
The shed'·deh شَدَّة is a tiny symbol that sits above a consonant to assert a double consonant, as in (rice: ruzz رُزّ). Instead of doubling the consonants, the sheddeh شَدَّة is placed on the first consonant and takes the place of the second consonant. Find and trace the sheddeh شَدَّة above these consonants:

دِّ   دُّ   دَّ   دّ

rice:	ruzz	رُزّ
make or do:	sew·wee'	سَوّي
sugar:	suk'·ker	سُكَّر
double consonant:	shed'·deh	شَدَّة
car ♀:	sey·yaa'·reh	سَيّارة
good/okay:	kwey'·yis	كْوَيِّس
teacher:	mu'·Ael·lim	مُعَلِّم

✎ Practice writing the sheddeh شَدَّة above these learned consonants:

طّ   يّ   لّ   وّ   زّ   رّ   ذّ   دّ

✎ Practice writing the sheddeh شَدَّة above these learned consonants and notice the use of the three short vowels above or below the sheddeh شَدّ:

طَّ   يَّ   لَّ   وَّ   زَّ   رَّ   ذَّ   دَّ

طُّ   يُّ   لُّ   وُّ   زُّ   رُّ   ذُّ   دُّ

طِّ   يِّ   لِّ   وِّ   زِّ   رِّ   ذِّ   دِّ

53

(3) meddeh مَدَّة آ as in (**A**dam: aa'·dem آدَم):
The med'·deh مَدَّة is a symbol that sits above the 'elif ألف and together they sound like the short English vowel ă, as in (**A**dam: aa'·dem آدَم). Also, it sits above the 'elif ألف inside words at the beginning of syllables as in (Koran: qur'·aan' قُرْآن). The meddeh مَدَّة is a minor symbol because it occurs in a limited number of words, mainly in the beginning of certain words or syllables. When possible, the symbol given to the meddeh in this book is ă or "aa". Find and trace on top of the meddeh مَدَّة above the 'elif ألف in these words:

ـآ   آ

Al:	ăl/ aal	آل
Alex:	ăl·iks/ aal'·iks	آلِكْس
Alley:	ăl·lee/ aal'·lee	آلِّي
Adam:	ădem/ aa'·dem	آدَم
August:	ăb/ aab	آب
March:	ă'·dhaar/ aa'·dhaar	آذار
a question:	soo'·ăl/ soo'·aal	سوآل
miseries:	me·ă'··see/ me·aa·see'	مآسي
The Koran:	'elqur·ăn'/ 'elqur·aan'	ألْقُرآن
I eat:	ă'·kul/ aa'·kul	آكُل
I take:	ă'·khudh/ aa'·khudh	آخُذ
now:	'el·ăn'/ 'el·aan'	ألآن
for now/till now:	lil·ăn'/ lil·aan'	لِلآن

✎ Practice writing the meddeh مَدَّة above all of these shapes of the 'elif ألف:

طلا   آذار   آلي   آل   لا   لا   ـآ   آ

طلا   آذر   آلي   آل   لا   لا   ـآ   آ

Chapter 3 — ʾelif meqSooreh: ألف مقصورة — tenween: تَنْوين

(1) ʾelif meqSooreh: ألف مَقصورة as in (to: ʾilaw إلى):
The ʾe·lif meq·Soo·reh is derived from the ʾelif but it has a slightly weaker sound; it sounds like the English vowel combination "aw" as in law, and it occurs <u>only</u> at the <u>end</u> of words in Arabic as in (music: moo·'see·qaw: موسيقى). The ʾelif meqSooreh ألف مَقصورة has two shapes that resemble the end and the isolated yaa' ياء but without any dots:

✎ Find and trace the attached and isolated shapes of the ʾelif meqSooreh ألِف مَقصورة in these words:

ى إلى   ى لَيْلى

music:	moo'·see·qaw	موسيقى
on:	Ae'·law	على
to:	ʾi'·law	إلى
youth:	Si'·baw	صِبى
What time:	me'·taw	مَتى
until:	He'·taw	حَتى
Nejwa:	nej'·waw	نَجْوى

The ʾe·lif meq·Soo'·reh ألِف مَقصورة occurs in certain common female names, as in:

ley'·law: لَيلى   nej'·waw: نَجْوى
sel'·waw: سَلْوى   hu'·daw: هُدى

✎ Practice writing the attached ى and the isolated ى shapes of the ʾelif meqSooreh ألِف مَقصورة:

ى ى ى ى ى ى   طي ى ى ى ى ى

لَيلى طى يى وى ذى زى ذى رى دى

The Arabic Alphabet for English Speakers

(2) Tenween تَنْوِين as in (thank you: shuk'·ren شُكْراً):
The ten·ween' تَنْوِين is an ending (suffix) that can have three different sounds. The first sound is like the "en" as in "taken" and in the Arabic word (thank you: shuk'·ren شُكْراً). The other two sounds are "un" as in (a book: ki·taa'·bun كِتابٌ) and "in" as in (a book: ki·taa'·bin كِتابٍ). The "un" and "in" endings involve the grammatical structure of sentences, not just words. It is best to study them at an advanced level of Arabic in the future. In this book, we are mainly concerned with the structure of words and simple sentences; thus, we will only study the "en" ending as in (thank you: shuk'·ren شُكْراً). When first hearing the "en" sound as in شُكْراً, one assumes that it is spelled with "en نْ." However, there is no "n" in these tenween endings. Instead, there is a double blip sitting above the 'elif as in (thank you: shuk'·ren شُكْراً) or above the final isolated hemzeh like this ءً as in (please: ri·jaa''·en رِجاءً). Notice that most of these words are adverbs:

أً   ـاً   لاً   لاً   ـاً   أً   ءً

شُكْراً   دائِماً   لَيْلاً   أوَّلاً   مَساءً

thanks:	shuk'·ra*a*en	شُكْراً
you welcome:	Aef'·wa*a*en	عَفْواً
very:	ji'·da*a*en	جِداً
please (not v.):	ri·jaa''·en	رِجاءً
a lot:	ke·thee'·ra*a*en	كَثيراً
in the morning:	Se·baa'·Ha*a*en	صَباحاً
always:	daa''i·ma*a*en	دائِماً
in the evening:	me·saa'·*aa*'en	مَساءً
nighttime:	ley'·la*a*en	لَيْلاً
a little:	qe·lee'·la*a*en	قَليلاً
first of all:	'ew''·we·la*a*en	أوَّلاً
tomorrow:	ghe 'den	غَداً

✎ Practice writing the tenween as it sits on the 'elif أَلِف or on the hemzeh هَمْزة:

أً   ـلاً   لَيْلاً   أوَّلاً   طِلاً   ءً   ـاءً

Chapter 4

ء : '   هَمْزة :hemzeh

داء ء   أَ أَب   أُ أُم   إِ إِلى

ـئ   زائِر   ـيء قارِيء   ؤ   لؤلؤ

hem′·zeh هَمْزة as in (physics: feez′·yaa' فيزياء):
The name of this symbol is hem′·zeh هَمْزة and it sounds like the sound of the glottal stop in the English word 'Uh 'Oh! It is most known in Arabic as the letter that rides on long vowels. The English symbol given to the hemzeh هَمْزة in this book is an apostrophe, as in 'e·laa·skeh ألاسْكا. There is an ongoing debate whether the hamzah هَمْزة is or is not a letter. However, it may be considered a letter when it can stand alone, as in (physics: feez′·yaa' فيزياء). The rest of the time, the hemzeh هَمْزة occurs riding on the long vowels and thus it may not be considered a letter. When the hemzeh rides on the long vowels, it suppresses their sounds; it makes them silent and then we only hear the hemzeh هَمْزة sound. The followings are the hemzeh هَمْزة positions alone and when riding above or below the three long Arabic vowels like this أ, إ, ؤ and ىء.

ء : '	as in physics:	feez·yaa'	فيزياء
aa'e: أَ	as in father:	*aa*'eb	أَب
aa'u: أُ	as in mother:	*aa*'um	أُم
aa'i: إِ	as in to:	*aa*'i·law	إِلى
u*oo*': ؤ	as in pearls:	lu*oo*'·lu*oo*'	لؤلؤ
oo'oo: ؤو	as in Raul:	raa·*oo*'ool	راؤول
ee'i: ـئ	as in visitor:	zaa·*ee*'ir	زائِر
ee'i·ee: ـئي	as in Zaire:	zaa·*ee*'eer	زائِر
i*ee*': يء	as in reader:	qaa·ri*ee*'	قارِيء

(1) Find the isolated hemzeh هَمْزَة as in (physics: feez'·yaa' فيزياء):

physics:	feez'·yaa'	فيزياء
chemistry:	keem'·yaa'	كيمياء
Sinai:	see'·naa'	سيناء
ailment:	daa'	داء
medication:	de·waa''	دَواء
desert:	SeH·raa''	صَحْراء
Sana:	Sen·Aaa''	صَنْعاء
ee or y:	yaa'	ياء
r:	raa'	راء
T:	Taa'	طاء
water:	maa'	ماء
mal:	soo'	سوء
filled:	mem·loo''	مَمْلوء
humankind:	mer'	مَرْء
evening:	me·saa''	مَساء
in the evening:	me·saa''·'en	مَساءً
behind:	we·raa''	وَراء
behind us:	we·raa''·'u·na*a*	وَرأنا
a plead with:	re·jaa''	رَجاء
please (not v.):	ri·jaa''·'en	رَجاءً
sky:	se·maa''	سَماء
his sky:	se·maa''·'u·hu	سَماءُهُ
our sky:	se·maa''·'u·na*a*	سَماءُنا
those:	haa'·oo'u·laa'	هَؤلاء

The Arabic Alphabet for English Speakers

(2) Find the hemzeh هَمْزَة that rides on top of the ('elif: aa أ), as in (America: *aa*'am·ree'·keh أَمْريكا):
Notice that the hemzeh suppresses the sounds of the 'elif, i.e. it makes the "aa" silent.

America:	*aa*'am·ree'·keh	أَمْريكا
Alaska:	*aa*'e·laa'·skeh	أَلاسْكا
the (prefix):	*aa*'el	أَلـ
aa:	*aa*'e·lif'	أَلِف
food:	*aa*'ekl	أَكْل
or:	*aa*'ew	أَو
the first:	*aa*'ew'·wel	أَوَل
days:	*aa*'ey·yaam'	أيام
asthma/crisis:	*aa*'ez'·meh	أَزْمَة
etiquette:	*aa*'e·te·ke*y*t	أَتَكِيت
father:	*aa*'eb	أَب
7-up:	se'·fin *aa*'eb	سَفِن آب
I study:	*aa*'ed'·rus	أَدْرُس
the east	*aa*'el·sherq'	ألْشَرْق
the middle:	*aa*'elew'·SeT	ألأَوْسَط
woman:	mer'·*aa*'eh	مَرْأَة
case/issue:	mes'·*aa*'e·leh	مِسْأَلَة
boredom:	se'·*aa*'em	سَأَم
he asked:	se'·*aa*'el	سَأَلَ
a person in crises:	me*aa*'·zoom'	مَأزوم

The Arabic Alphabet for English Speakers

(3) Find the hemzeh هَمْزَة followed by vowels other than the (fetHeh), as in (mother: *aa*'um أُمْ):

mother:	*aa*'**um**	أُمْ
he saw:	re·*aa*'**aw**'	رَأى
merciful:	re*aa*·'**oo**f'	رَؤوف
Jordan:	*aa*'**ur**'·dun	أُرْدُن
Ohio:	*aa*'**ō**'·haa·yōo	أوْهايو
Orlando:	*aa*'**ō**r'·laan·dōo	أوْرلانْدو
oven:	*aa*'**ō**'·fin	أوفِن
opera:	*aa*'**ō**op'·reh	أوبْرا

(4) Find the hemzeh هَمْزَة riding under the long vowel ('elif) and still suppressing the sound of ('elif), as in (if: *aa*'i'·dhaa إذا):

Istanbul:	*aa*'i̱s·Ten·bool'	إسْطَنْبول
English:	*aa*'i̱n·ki·lee'·zee	إنْكليزي
The English language:	*aa*'el·*aa*'i̱n·ki·lee·zi·yeh	أَلإنْكليزيَة
if:	*aa*'i̱'·dhaa	إذا
except:	*aa*'i̱'·laa	إلا
the one that:	*aa*'i̱l·lee'	إلْلي
that (as in said that):	*aa*'i̱n'·ne	إنَّ
give:	*aa*'i̱·dee'	إدي
tell a tale:	*aa*'i̱r·wee'	إرْوي
fold (v.):	*aa*'i̱T·wee'	إطْوي

(5) Find the hemzeh هَمْزَة riding on top of the long vowel (oo: waaw و), as in (Raul: raaʹ·*oo*ʹool راؤول):
Notice that the hemzeh suppresses the sound of "oo"; it makes it silent:

pearls:	luʹ*oo*ʹ·lu*oo*ʹ	لؤلؤ
conference:	muʹ*oo*ʹ·te·mer	مؤتَمَر
those (formal):	ha̱aʹ·*oo*ʹu·laaʹ	هَؤُلاء
Raul:	raaʹ·*oo*ʹool	راؤول
responsible:	mes·*oo*ʹoolʹ	مَسْؤول

(6) Find the hemzeh هَمْزَة riding above the long vowel (yaaʹ: ee), as in (Zaire: zaaʹ··ʹeer زائير):
The hemzeh sits above the yaaʹ making it silent and it must be followed by a vowel when not at the end of words. It is said that the hemzeh sits on the yaaʹ like it's sitting on a chair: ئـ ـئـ ـئ ئ

always:	daaʹ·*ee*ʹi·men	دائِماً
continuous:	daaʹ·*ee*ʹim	دائِم
Algeria/islands:	je·zaaʹ·*ee*ir	جَزَئِر
visitor:	zaaʹ·*ee*ʹir	زائِر
Zaire:	zaaʹ·*ee*ʹeer	زائير
reader:	qaaʹ·ri*ee*ʹ	قارِيء
bad:	seyʹ·y*ee*ʹ	سَيِّيء
bad quality:	re·di*ee*ʹ	رَدييء
seen:	mer·*ee*ʹeeʹ	مَرْئي

**Read aloud the ء with other learned letters and symbols five times per page and focus on the hemzeh. Do not write yet; you must first read a language aloud before you begin to write it:

أَلْدال   دال   أَلْطاء   طاء   أَلْذال   ذال   داء   أَلْراء   راء

أَلْأَوْلاد   أَوْلاد   لِلْأَبَد   أَلْأَبَد   أَبَداً   أَبَد   أَوَّل   أَلْواو   واو

أَوى   وَإِد   رَأى   لِلْأَطْوار   أَلْإِطْوار   أَطْوار   لِلْأَوْلاد

وَإِذا   إِذْ   وَإِلا   إِلى   إِطْوي   إِرْوي   طَأْطَأْ   يَأْوي

لِلْأُرْدُن   أَلْأُرْدُن   أُرْدُن   لِلْأُم   اَلْأُم   أُم   إِدي   إِلّي

راؤول   اَلْأَرْز   أَرْز   أُري   إِلّي   أَذْوي   أُداري   أُداوي

وائل   طائِل   زائِل   يُؤْلِم   بُؤْرَة   بُؤْبُؤ   لُؤْلُؤ   مَسْؤول

لِئَلا   طاطيء   رَدييء   طواريء   طاريء   طلائل   طائِل

رَدييء   زائِر   زائِر

The Arabic Alphabet for English Speakers

✒ Practice writing the hemzeh alone and in words:

أَوْ　أُ　أَ　إِ　رِئ　لاء　طاء　راء　ء　ء　ء

يَأْوِي　يَأ　إذا　إِ　إِ　إِ　إِ　أُرْز　أُ　أُ　أَ

ئـ　لُؤْلُؤ　وَ　رَاؤُول　وُؤ　أَلَا　لِإِ　لِلإِ　ـلا　ـلا　لا

راء　طاريء　يء　طيء　ليء　لِئَلا　ئـ　زائير

اَلدّال　اَلذال　ذال　اَلطاء　طاء　اَلدّاء　داء　اَلرّاء

رأى　أَطْوار　لِلأَوْلاد　أَوْلاد　لِلأَبَد　أَبَداً　أَوَّل　اَلْواو

اَللّي　إذا　إلا　إلى　اِطْوِي　اِرْوِي　طَأْطَأَ　يَأْوِي　أَوى

يُؤلِم　لُؤْلُؤ　رَاؤُول　الأُرْز　أَداوي　أُرْدُن　أَلأم　أُمّ　إدي

زائير　لِئَلا　طَوَاريء　رَدِيء　طَلائِل　وَائِل　طائِل　زائِل

| Chapter 5 | Numbers 0-20 | | أرقام |

Read and write these 0-20 Arabic numbers from right to left←

English	Transliteration	Arabic name	Number
zero:	Sifr	صِفْر	٠
one:	waa'·Hid	واحِد	١
two:	'ith·neen'	إثْنين	٢
three:	the·laa'·theh	ثَلاثَة	٣
four:	'er'·be·Aeh	أرْبَعَة	٤
five:	khem'·seh	خَمْسِة	٥
six:	si'·teh	سِتَة	٦
seven:	seb'·Aeh	سَبْعَة	٧
eight:	the·maan'·yeh	ثَمانْيَة	٨
nine:	tis'·Aeh	تِسْعَة	٩
ten:	Aesh'·reh	عَشْرَة	١٠
eleven:	'iH·daa' Ae'·sher	إحْدى عَشَر	١١
twelve:	'ith·naa' Aesher	إثْنى عَشَر	١٢
thirteen:	the·laa'·thet Aesher	ثَلاثَة عَشَر	١٣
fourteen:	'er'·be·Aet Aesher	أرْبَعَة عَشَر	١٤
fifteen:	khem'·set Aesher	خَمْسَة عَشَر	١٥
sixteen:	si'·tet Aesher	سِتَة عَشَر	١٦
seventeen:	seb'·Aet Aesher	سَبْعَة عَشَر	١٧
eighteen:	the·maa'·nyet Aesher	ثَمانْيَة عَشَر	١٨
nineteen:	tis'·Aet Aesher	تِسْعَة عَشَر	١٩
twenty:	Aish·roon'	عِشْرون	٢٠

Summary of the Nine Arabic Symbols

short vowels: di: دِ   du: دُ   de: دَ

long vowels: dee: دي   doo: دو   daa: دا

'elif meqsooreh: aw: ى

meddeh: ă/aa: آ

sikoon: as in: dl دْل

sheddeh: as in: dd دّ

tenween: as in: den داً

Summary of All Learned Letters and Symbols

The Arabic Alphabet for English Speakers

y or ee				ياء	d			دال
ي	ـي	ـيـ	يـ		ـد			د
دي	آلي	طير	ياء		ديدي			دال
l				لام	aa			ألِف
ل	ـل	ـلـ	لـ		ـا			ا
دال	طَويل	بْلوز	لَيْزَر		طار			راديو
T				طاء	oo or w			واو
ط	ـط	ـطـ	طـ		ـو			و
واط	بَط	يَطير	طاء		طَويل			واو
z				زاي	r			راء
	ـز	ز				ـر	ر	ر
	يَزول	زاي				يَريد	راء	
hemzeh				هَمْزة	dh			ذال
ء	ؤ	يء	ـئـ	أ إ أ			ـذ	ذ
							لَذيذ	ذال
Other		حركات وسكون وشَدة ومدة وألف مقصورة			tenween			تَنْوين
ى ىَ	آ	دّ	دْ	دِ دُ دَ		ءٍ أً أٌ أً	لاً لاَ	ـلاً

The Arabic Alphabet for English Speakers

Practice Test of Parts One and Two
Translate these sounds and words into Arabic letters:

doo	daa	di	du	de

dhaa	dhi	dhu	dhe	dee

ri	ru	re	dhee	dhoo

zu	ze	ree	roo	raa

we	zee	zoo	zaa	zi

wee	woo	waa	wi	wu

dhaal	raa'	daal	waaw	zaa'

to: 'ilaw	no: laa	if: 'idhaa	the: 'el	or: 'ew

rice: ruzz	'elruzz	doolaar	'iTaalee	widaad

zaaee'eer	loou'loou'	visitor: zaa'ir	ledheedh	leyzer

raazee	raaoo'ool	weeT	waaT	yeTeer

Taa'	yaa'	ălee	deyzee	tall: Teweel

yereed	yezool	'eldoolaar	leylaaen	redhaadh

if: 'idhaa	raadyoo	deeloor	Taar	rid

waalee	leyree	rooy	night: leyl	'elleyl

zoozoo	daawree	'ulee	rud	wez

PART THREE
Six More Letters

Name	Symbol	As in	Isolated	End	Middle	Beginning
baa': باء	b	bank	ب	ـب	ـبـ	بـ
meem: ميم	m	may	م	ـم	ـمـ	مـ
Haa': هاء	h	his	ه	ـه	ـهـ	هـ
noon: نون	n	noon	ن	ـن	ـنـ	نـ
jeem: جيم	j	jet	ج	ـج	ـجـ	جـ
seen: سين	s	sit	س	ـس	ـسـ	سـ

Isolated	End	Middle	Beginning
ب	ـب	ـبـ	بـ
م	ـم	ـمـ	مـ
ه	ـه	ـهـ	هـ
ن	ـن	ـنـ	نـ
ج	ـج	ـجـ	جـ
س	ـس	ـسـ	سـ

Chapter 1   b: ب   baa': باء

This Arabic letter name is baa' باء and it sounds like the English "b" as in "bat". The letter baa' باء is a consonant and it is given the symbol "b" in this book, as in (robe: rōob روب). Note that because there is no "p" in the Arabic alphabet, Arabic speakers may say "p" but write "b." For instance, Arabic speakers may say the "p" in "piano" but write bee·yaa·nōo: بيانو. The baa' باء has four shapes: beginning ﺑ, middle ﺒ, end ﺐ, and isolated ب:

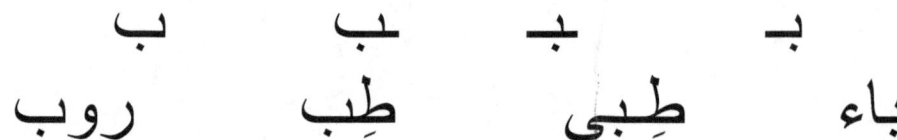

❶ Learning Step One: Read and pay attention to the four shapes of baa' باء. Read horizontally:

baa':	باء	door:	باب
blouse:	بْلوز	Buddha	بوذا
bottle:	بُطُل	hero:	بَطَل
Rabat:	رِباط	Brazil:	بَرازيل
raisins:	زِبيب	powder:	باوْدِر
daddy:	بابا	grandma:	بيبي
robe:	روب	good/okay:	طَيِّب
chest drawers:	دولاب	female name:	رَباب
thaws:	يَذوب	thawed:	ذاب
flies (n.):	ذُباب	bear:	دُب
central part:	لُب	behind/after:	وَراء
fox:	ذِئب	foxes:	ذِئاب
ducks:	بَط	night:	لَيل
the night:	أَلْليل	in (prefix):	بِ
in the night:	بِأَلْليل	in a bottle:	بِبُطِل
the one that:	إِلّي	September:	أَيْلول
physician:	طَبيب	male name:	لَبيب
first:	أَوَّل	first of all	أَوَّلاً
lord:	رَب	my lord:	رَبي

The Arabic Alphabet for English Speakers

soup	سوب	Oh my lord:	يا رَبي
father:	أَب	August:	آب
student:	طالِب	the father:	أَلأَب
asks for:	يَطْلُب	a request:	طَلَب

زور بابا   زور لَبيب   زور رَباب   زور أَلرِباط   أَلبَرازيل زور

زور أَلطُلاب   زور أَلطالِب   زور أَلأَب   زور بيبي

❷ **Learning Step Two:** First read the letter baa' باء with other learned letters aloud many times and focus on its four shapes. Do not write yet; you must first read a language aloud before you begin to write it: ←

بيبي   بي   بي   بوبو   بو   بو   بابا   با   با

باب   بيباب   بيبا   بيبا   بيب   بيب   بيبو   بيبو   بيبي

يَذوب   ذاب   يَباب   رَباب   باب   بيب   بيبوب

باوْدِر   رِباط   بوذا   بْلوز   باء   زِبيب   طِبول   طَبل

ذِئب   زِرياب   ذُباب   لُب   دُب   وَراء   بَرازيل   روب

طالب   طُلاب   طَيَّب   بَطَل   بُطُل   باوْدِر   بيبي   ذِئاب

أَوَّل   إلّي   أَلّلَيْل   لَيْل   لَبيب   طَبيب   يَطْلُب   طَلَب

بَط   أوبْرا   يا رَبي   رَبي   رَبْ   بَريد   يَريد   أَيْلول   أَوَّلاً

بِب   بيب   بُب   بو   بَب   باب   يابا   اَلأَب   أَب   آبْ

71

Part Three

❸ **Practice writing these four shapes of the letter ب and notice the Tahoma font bellow making it look more like handwritten text:**

ب بـ ـبـ ـب

ب بـ ـبـ ـب

باء طِبي طِب روب

←
بـ بـ بـ بـ بـ بط بـ بـ بـ بـ بـ طبل

ب ب ب ب ب طب ب ب ب ب ب باب

با بو بي ذيب رَب دُب أب آب ذاب دولاب

طِب ببب لَبيب لَبيبَة زور لَبيب وَلَبيبَة زور بيبي

باب باء بْلوز بوذا طالِب باوِدر بابا بيبي بَط

طَبيب ألْروب ألْلُب دَأوب دَأبَ ذِئب ذِئاب

بَرازيل رِباط طَبيب طَيِّب روب

زور أَلْبَرازيل زور أَلْرِباط زور رَباب زور لَبيب

72

❹ Pick the correct shape of the letter ﺏ to fill in these blanks:

ب   ب   ب   ب

ب   ب   ب   ب

←

ـــا   ـــاـــا   أَلْـــا   ـــا   طا   طَيّ   ـــرَ   دُـــ

ط   ـــاوْدِر   آـــ   أَـــو   زيـــرا   ـــيـــي   ـــرَي

رو   ـــ   ـــ   ـــا   ألْبا   ـــُـــ   ألْـــ   طالِـــ   ألْطالِـــ

طُلا   ـــ   ـــلوز   ألْـــلوز   أوـــرا   ـــرازيل   ـــريد

طبيـــ   لَبيـــ   طَيّـــ   ـــيـــو   آـــ   أـــ   دُـــ

ألأَـــ   لِلأَـــ   طَيّـــ   ـــاـــ   لا   ـــ   دولا

زِرْيا   ـــ   ـــيَد   ذِئـــ   ذِئا   دأـــ   داوـــ

طَلَـــ   ـــ   يَطْلُـــ   طُلا   ـــرازيل   رِـــاط

طِـــ   لَـــيب   لَـــيبَة   زور لَبيـــ   ولَبيـــة   زور بيـــي

73

Chapter 2 — m: م — meem: ميم

This Arabic letter name is meem ميم and it sounds like the English "m" as in "moon". The letter meem is a consonant and it is given the symbol "m" in this book as in (mom: maa·maa ماما). The meem ميم has four shapes: beginning مـ, middle ـمـ, end ـم, and isolated م. There is a slight difference between the last two shapes of the printed م ـم and the handwritten م ـم. See the four shapes of meem alone and in words:

❶ Learning Step One: Read these words aloud and pay attention to the four shapes of meem ميم and read horizontally:

meem:	ميم	laam:	لام
Madrid:	مَدْريد	Malaysia:	مالي
mine:	مالي	mother:	ماما
tomatoes:	طَماطِم	a mother:	أُم
my mother:	أُمّي	style:	موديل
water:	مَي	airport:	مَطار
while:	لَمّا	always:	دائِماً
rain:	مَطَر	rainy:	مُمْطِر
outcaste:	مَمبوذ	stretched:	مَمْطوط
in crisis:	مأزوم	captured:	مَلْزوم
nations:	أُمَم	mummy:	مَوْمِياء
bananas:	موز	Italian:	إيطالي
European:	أورُبي	stuffed grape leaves:	دولْما
day: yōom	يوم	today:	إلْيوم
blame (v.):	لوم	blame ♀:	لومي
peace:	سَلام	mirror:	مَرايا
beside:	يَم	not:	مو
not in my hand:	مو بيدي	penny:	مَليم

beside me:	يَمي	throw (v.):	إرْمي
mile:	ميل	in front of:	أَمام
imam:	إِمام	mean (adj.):	لَئيم
blood:	دَم	filled up:	مَمْلوء
Adam:	آدَم	good person:	آدَمي
visit (v):	زور	visit (v.) ♀:	زوري
lasted:	دام	days:	أيْام
pain/ache:	أَلَم	my pain:	أَلَمي
pains (plural):	آلآم	bitter:	مُر

Part Three

❷ Read the meem ميم with other learned letters aloud, five times per each page:

←

ما ما ماما ماما مو مو مومو مومو مو مي مي

ميمي ميمي ميم زوما روما لوما بِرْما دولما لوم

لومي لِم لِمي طِمي طِم ذِمي ذِم أُم أمي يَم يَمي

إرْم إرْمي ديم ديمي ميم وَميم دَميم يَميم

لَئيم زِمام أمام إمام لام يَم ميل دَم يَم يَمي

مَمْلوء مَطَر مُمْطِر مَمْطوط لَم أُم أُمْمَم آدَم

لوم دوم مالي مَطار مَي مو مومِياء أورُبي

موديل إيطالي موز يوم إِليوم بومْبَي مَدْريد أمام

ماما مو بيدي زوري مَزوري مَلْزوم مأزوم يَم لَم

بلَم دام أيام لام آلآم أَلَم ألَمي مُر لَما دائِما

مَلّيم زم زمْزم ذِم ذِمْذِم رِم رِمْرِم دِم دِمْدِم

ممام ممم زوري أَلْمَدريد زوري أَلْبَرازيل زوري آدَم زوري

أَلأُم زوري أَلْمَدريد إِليوم زوري أَلْبَرازيل إِليوم زوري آدَم

إِليوم زوري أَلآم إِليوم زوري أَلأُم دائِماً دائِماً زوري أَلأُم

76

❸ Practice writing these four shapes of the letter ميم:

مـ   ـمـ   ـم   م

Handwritten↓

ميل   دائِماً   أَلَمْ   آدَمُ

مـ ـمـ ـم ما   ـمـ ـمـ ـمـ لَمّا

م م م م ميم   م م م م أُمْ

مام ماما مومو مي ميمي ميل روما لوما

ميمي بوما بزْما دولما مامي لومي لِم ذِم

مام طام بام يام لام أُم أُمي يَم يَمي ذِم

ميم مَدْريد موز ريم موديل يوم مَطار مِرايا

أَلَمْ مُر لَمّا دائِماً زامْبْيا مَمْلوء مُمْطِر ميمي

لوما بوما بزْما دولما مامي لومي لِم ذِم

زوري ألْمَدْريد إلْيوم   زوري ألْبَرازيل إلْيوم   زوري آدَم إلْيوم

زوري ألأُم إلْيوم   زوري ألأُم دائِماً   دائِماً زوري ألأَلَم

❹ Pick the correct shape of the letter م to fill in these blanks:

مـ   ـمـ   ـم   م

مُ   ـَمْ   ـِمـ   ـَمْ
ميل   دائماً   أَلَم   آدَم

←
ـا_ـا   _ـو_و   رو_ـا   بِر_ـا   دول_ـا   ما_ي   ما_ي
_ـيمي   مي_ـي   لـ_ـي   لِ_   ذِ_   ذِ_ي   مـ_ـي
إلـ_ـام   رو_ـا   _ـوز   _ـدْريد   _ـوز   زا_بيا   _ـي
ـودَيل   يو   _طار   _ـرايا   _ـزوري   _ـاليزيا   دو_
دَ_يم   لئـ_   _دَ_   زِمْزِ_   أُمَـ_   آد_   لو_   لَ_
مَوْ_ياء   إِ_ـام   _ـمْلوء   آد_   آدَ_ي   بو_بَي   ذِم
_ـطَر   مـ_طِر   _مطوط   لئـ_   مأزو_   آلا
أَلَـ_   أَلْأَلَـ_   دائـ_ـاً   لًـ_ـا   _ـدا   _ـيل   دا
_ـيل   ـا_ـا   دائـ_ـاً   أَلَـ_   آدَ_

Chapter 3   h: ‍هـ   haa': هاء

This Arabic letter name is haa' هاء and it sounds like the English "h" as in "had". The haa' هاء is a consonant and it is given the symbol "h" in this book as in (Heather: he·dher هَذَر). The haa' هاء and all the remaining Arabic letters have four shapes; beginning هـ, middle ـهـ, end ـه, and isolated ه. Note that the "eh" ـة at the end of some words is used in spoken but not in written Arabic; the "eh" often turns into "et" in written Arabic but it is still pronounced "eh", as in مُهِمَة. There are details about the suffix "eh" or "et" when you study the (ة) (tight t: taa' mer·boo'·Teh تاء مَربوطة) in the "تاء" chapter. See the four shapes of haa' alone and in words:

❶ Read these words aloud slowly. This ending (et ـة) is pronounced (eh ـه), as in (potato: beTaaTet بطاطة) that is pronounced (potato: beTaaTeh بطاطه). In most words, the "eh" indicates that a word has a female gender. Unlike English, the "h" does have a sound at the end of words:

Heather:	هَذَر	Ohio:	أوهايو
salad:	زَلاطَة	potatoes:	بطاطَة
Malta:	مالْطَة	Harlem:	هارْلِم
med'·deh:	مَدَّة	hem'·zeh:	هَمْزَة
protagonist:	بَطَل	heroine:	بَطَلَة
prince:	أَمير	princes:	أَميرَة
important:	مُهِم	important ♀:	مُهِمَة
delicious:	لَذيذ	delicious ♀:	لَذيذَة
escape (n.):	هروب	the escape:	أَلْهِروب
yes (e & m):	أَيْوَه	let's:	يَلّه
sound of sigh:	آه	they blamed him:	لاموه
they threw him:	رَموه	father:	أَبو
his father:	أَبوه	her father:	أَبوها
water (f):	ماء	his water:	ماءه
her water:	ماءُها	behind:	وَراء
behind him:	وَراءَه	behind her:	وَراءَها
this: haa'·dhaa	هَذا	this ♀: haa'·dhi*h*	هَذِه

she:	هِيَ	he:	هُوَ
for him:	لَهُ	for her:	لَها
in it:	بِهِ	in it ♀:	بِها
his necktie:	رِباطُه	her blouse:	بْلوزَها
his mother:	أُمُه	her mother:	أَمَها
night:	لَيل	one night:	لَيلَه
female name:	ليلى	pyramids:	أَهرام
one pyramid:	هَرَم	welcome:	أَهْلا
gold:	ذَهَب	he went (f):	ذَهَب
hello:	هَلو	shrewd:	داهِية
spice:	بَهار	crescent:	هِلال
flowers:	وَرْد	flower ♀:	وَرْدَة
airplane ♀:	طَيّارَة	needle ♀:	إِبْرَة
circle ♀:	دائِرة	lamp ♀:	لَمْبة
crisis ♀:	أَزْمَة	guide ♀:	دَليلَة

❷ Read the haa' هاء with other learned letters aloud, five times per page:

ها ها هاها هاها هو هو هوهو هوهو هِيَ هِي

هيهي هيهي هيهو بيهو هاه ذاه أَطْلاَنْطَة

مالْطَة بَطاطَة زَلاطَة هايْدي أوهايو آه داه طاه

إِياه زاه واه أُماه أَباه رَباه لاموه رَموه ذَبوه

أَبوه به بِهِ زاهِية داهِية راهِية لاهِية بَطَل

بَطَلَة وَراء وَراءه هُوَ هَلو هِروب أَلْهروب

رِباطُهُ رِباط بْلوزَها بْلوز ماؤُها ماء أبوها أبو

هَذَر هِيَ هَذِه بِها طَها لَها هو وَرْدُهُ وَرد

طَيَّارَة طَهارَة مَهارَة دائِرَة باهِرَة ماهِرَة هالَة

أَميرَة أَمير مُهِمَة مُهِم لَذيذَة هَذا يَلَّه إِبْرَة

هاء بِهِ لَهُ لَيْلَة لَيل أَهْرام هَرَم أوهايو

أُمّها بَهار لَمْبَة أَهْلا هَلاهِل هَلْهَل ذَهَب ذَهَب

هِلال أَزْمَة مَدَة هَزيلَة دَليلَة رَزيلَة لَها بِها

هُهوه ههاه هههِ هيم هُم هوم هَم هام

هَذِهِ مالْطِة هَذِهِ أَطْلانْطَة ههههههه هههههه هِهيه

هَذِهِ ديلايْلَة هَذِهِ لَيلى هَذِهِ هَذَر هَذِهِ أَلْبَرازيل هَذَهِ أوهايو

هَذِهِ بَطاطَة هَذِهِ أُمُّها هَذِهِ أُمّي هَذِهِ أُمُّه هَذِهِ أُم

هَذِهِ زَلاطَة لَذيذَة هَذِهِ بَطاطَة لَذيذَة هَذِهِ لَذيذَة هَذِهِ زَلاطَة

هَذِهِ هَذِهِ لَمْبَة هَذِهِ وَرْدَة هَذِهِ دائِرَة هَذِهِ طَيَّارَة

هَذِهِ أَميرَة هَذِهِ هَمْزَة هَذِهِ مَدَّة هَذِهِ أَميرَة هَذِهِ أَزْمَة إِبْرَة

هَذَهِ أُم مُهِمَة هَذِهِ أَميرَة داهِية هَذِهِ أَميرَة بَطَلَة مُهِمَة

هَذا هَذا أَبْ مُهِم هَذا أَبْ هَذِهِ أُم داهِية هَذِهِ أُم بَطَلَة

هَذا أَمير هَذا أَمير مُهِم هَذا أَمير هَذا أَبْ داهِية أَبْ بَطَل

هَذا أَمير داهِية بَطَل

❸ Practice writing the four shapes of the letter هاء:

ه ـه ـهـ هـ

أَبوه هـ أُمُه ـه مُهِم ـهـ هِي هـ

لَها ـه ـه ـه ـه ـه هاء هـ هـ هـ هـ

هَذِه ه ه ه ه أُمُه ـه ـه ـه ـه ـه

ها هاها هو هوهو هي هيهي هيهو بيهو هاء

هو هام هايدي أوهايو داهِية زاهِية به بَطَلَة

آه داه طاه واه هاه رَموه أبوه أيوَه هِلال

هِروب ألهروب لَها بها مَها أمَها هَذِه هِي

هَذَر هَمْزَة بَهار لَذيذَة وَرْدَة أميرَة إبْرَة

ماهِرَة باهِرَة دائِرَة مَهارَة طَهارَة طَيّارَة

مَدَّة أزْمَة رَذيلَة دَليلَة هَزيلَة يَله هَلو

هَلْهل ذَهَب ذَهَب هِم هَرَم أهْرام هَذا

لَه بهِ مُهِم مُهِمَة بَطاطَة زَلاطَة طَماطَة

مالْطَة أطْلانْطَة لَمْبَة أهْلا لَيْلَة لَيْلى بها

The Arabic Alphabet for English Speakers

❹ Pick the correct shape of the letter هاء to fill in these blanks:

ه   ه   ه   ه

ـه   ة   ـهـ   ـه

ـاء   ـاـا   ـو   ـوـو   ـيـي   ـام   ـايْدي

أوـايو   هيـو   ـيهو   آ   ذا   طا   إيا   وا

ها   أما   رَبا   لامو   رَمو   أبو   بِـ   وَراءُ

ـروب   ألـِـروب   ـوَ   إلـاء   ليـ   رِباطُ

ماءُـ   ماءُـ   بلوزـا   لـا   بِـا   يلـ   ـلو   لـهل

بَـار   ذَـبَ   ـم   ـرم   أـرام   ـذا   لَـ   بِـ

أمَـا   ـذِه   ـيَ   ـذَر   أـلا   مُـم   ـارْزِم   إلـام

هههو   هَوى   ـههوه   هها   هه_ـه

➤ Notice that the final (haa' ه) turns to a (t ة) called تاء مَربوطة with the two dots above it; more explanations will be available when you study the letter "t" تاء:

دائِرة   بَطَلة   ماهِيَّة   لاهِيَة   داهِيَة   زاهِيَة

لَيْلَة   أزْمَة   مَدَّة   إبْرَة   أميرَة   وَرْدَة   لَذيذة   طَيّارة

أطْلانْطَة   طَماطَة   بَطاطَة   مالْطَة   مُهِمَة   لَمْبَة

➤ Fill in these blanks with the final "h" sound that is spelled with a special "t" called تاء مَربوطة:

دائِرـ   بَطَلـ   ماهِيَّـ   لاهِيَـ   داهِيَـ   زاهِيَـ

أزْمَـ   مَدَّـ   إبْرَـ   أميرَـ   وَرْدَـ   لَذيذَـ   طَيّارـ

طَماطَـ   بَطاطَـ   مالْطَـ   مُهِمَـ   لَمْبَـ   لَيْلَـ

83

Chapter 4   ن :n   نون :noon

Part Three

This Arabic letter name is noon نون and it sounds like the English "n" as in "in." The letter noon نون is a consonant and it is given the symbol "n" in this book as in (lemons: ley·moon لَيْمون). The noon نون has four shapes: beginning نـ, middle ـنـ, end ـن, and isolated ن:

ن	ـن	ـنـ	نـ
نون	مين	ينام	نام

❶ Read these Arabic words aloud slowly focusing on the four shapes of noon نون:

a lemon:	لَيْمونَة	lemons:	لَيْمون
Lebanese:	لِبْناني	Lebanon:	لُبْنان
Iran:	إيران	Lebanese ♀:	لِبْنانِيَة
Iranian ♀:	إيرانِيَة	Iranian:	إيراني
Indian:	هِنْدي	India:	ألْهِنْد
Indians:	هِنود	Indian ♀:	هِنْدِية
Nairobi:	نايْروبي	nanny:	نانا
Arizona:	أريزونَة	Jordan:	ألأَرْدُن
Atlanta:	أطْلانْطَة	Tanzania:	طَنْزانْيَة
London:	لَنْدَن	Orlando:	أورْلانْدو
Romania:	رومانْيَة	Yemen:	ألْيَمَن
mud:	طين	beads:	نِمنِم
millionaire ♀:	مِلْيونَيرَة	millionaire:	مِلْيونَير
time/history:	زَمان	potatoes ♀:	بَطاطَة
son of:	بِن	from:	مِن
where:	وَين	who:	مين
flames:	نيران	fire:	نار
without me:	بِدوني	without:	بِدون
two rivers:	نَهْرَين	river:	نَهْر
two blouses:	بْلوزَين	blouse:	بْلوز

two pyramids: هَرَمَين	pyramid: هَرَم
two pants: بَنْطَلونَين	pants: بَنْطَلون
two boys: وَلَدَين	one boy: وَلَد
two n's: نونَين	one n: نون
I: أنا	now (f): ألآن
because I am: لأنَّني	because: لأنَّهُ
thankful ♀: مَمْنونَة	thankful: مَمْنون
clubs: نَوادي	social club: نادي
foxes: نِمور	fox: نِمر
our religion: دينَنا	religion: دين
night & day: لَيل نَهار	their religion: دينْهُم
sleep (n.): nōom نوم	here: هُنا
I sleep: أنام	sleep (v.): نام
we sleep: نَنام	he sleeps: يَنام
they sleep: يَنامون	sleep (v.) ♀: نامي

❷ Read aloud the noon نون with other learned letters, five times per page:

نا نا نانا نانا نو نو نونو نونو ني ني

نيني نيني ناني راني هيني ديني ويني

طَنْزانْيِة أورْلانْدو أطْلانْطَة اَلأُرْدِن أريزونا نايروبي

تايْوان لُبْنان لُبْناني لُبْنانِيَة أليابان ياباني يابانِيَة

أَلْهِنْد هِنْدي هِنْدِيَة أَلْيَمَن يَمَنِية نون نون

نون نونَين بَنْطَلون بَنْطَلونَين وَلَد وَلَدَين

نَهْر   نَهْرَين   بْلوز   بْلوزَين   هَرَم   هَرَمَين

مين   وَين   طين   رَن   بان   هان   لان   زَمان   آن

أَلأَوان   اَلأَن   لِلآن   آني   واني   ماني   هاني   وَلاني

هِنْري   نائِل   نور   نوري   نِهاد   لينا   زينا   فاتِن   نينا

بِدون   بِدوني   إنَّ   أنا   إنَّني   لِإنَّه   أَلأَنَّني   إِذْني

مَمْنون   مِمْنونَة   مِلْيوْنَير   مِلْيوْنَيرَة   نِمْنِم   نِمِر   نِمور

نار   نيران   نادي   نَوادي   مِن   لنْدَن   هُنا   نَهْر أَلْنيل

لَيْمون   نَهار وَلَيل   دين   دينُنا   دينُهم   بِن   نوم   نام   أنام

يَنام   نَنام   يَنامون   نام   أنا لُبْناني   أنا إيراني   أنا

هِنْدي   أنا أُرْدني   أنا نايروبي   أنا مِن لُبْنان   أنا مِن إيران

أنا مِن إلْهِنْد   أنا مِن هُنا   أنا مِن الأُرْدِن   أنا مِن نايروبي   أنا

مِن أَريزونا   أنا مِن لَنْدَن   أنا مِن إلْيَمَن   أنا مِن أَطْلانْطَة   أنا مِن

أورلانْدو   أنا مِن طَنْزانيَة   أنا من رومانيا   أنا مِن إلْدُنْيا   أنا

لُبْنانيَة ♀   أنا إيرانيَة ♀   أنا هِنْديَة ♀   أنا طَنْزانيَة ♀

The Arabic Alphabet for English Speakers

❸ Learning Step Three: Practice writing these four shapes of the letter نون:

ن　ـن　ـنـ　نـ

Handwritten↓

ن　ـن　ـنـ　نـ
نون　طَن　هُنا　نور

←

نـ　نـ　نـ　نـ　نا　　　نـ　نـ　نـ　نـ　هِند

_____

نـ　ن　ن　ن　بُن　　　ن　ن　ن　ن　رَن

_____

نا　نانا　نو　نونو　ناني　ني　نيني　ديني　وَيني　وينو

_____

دَينو　دين　مين　طين　مِن　وَين　وَيني　وينو

_____

نونين　رَن　بان　نونو　هان　لان　زَمان　ماني　لُبْنان

_____

لُبْناني　هاني　بدوني　واني　لاني　ياباني　يابان

_____

ألآن　آن　ألآوان　آذار　آذان　نار　نيران　نور

_____

نوري　نوم　نِمور　نِمِم　مَمْنون　مَمْنونَة　هُنا　دينُنا

_____

87

| بدون | لِأَنَني | إنَّني | إنَّ | إذْني | آذاني | آني | دينُهُم |

| نايروبي | أريزونا | نائي | مائِل | زائِل | أنا نائِل | لَيْمون |

| هِنْدي | الأُرْدُن | أطْلانْطَة | أورْلانْدو | طَنْزانيا | تايْوان |

| نَهْر النيل | مين | نادي | لَيْمون | بدون | لِأَنَني | هِنْدِية |

| أنا نايروبي | أنا أُرْدِني | أنا هِنْدي | أنا إيراني | أنا لُبْناني |

| أنا مِن هُنا | أنا مِن الْهِنْد | أنا مِن إيران | أنا مِن لُبْنان |

| أنا مِن لَنْدَن | أنا مِن أريزونا | أنا مِن نايروبي | أنا مِن الأُرْدِن |

| أنا مِن أورْلانْدو | أنا مِن أطْلانْطَة | أنا مِن الْيَمَن |

| أنا مِن الدُّنْيا | أنا مِن رومانيا | أنا مِن طَنْزانِية |

| أنا طَنْزانِية | أنا هِنْدية | أنا إيرانية | أنا لُبْنانِية |

The Arabic Alphabet for English Speakers

❹ Pick the correct shape of the letter نون to fill in these blanks:

ن   ـن   ـنـ   نـ
ن   ـن   ـنـ   نـ
نون   طَن   هُنا   نور

←
ـاَنا   ـوـو   ـيـ   ـيـي   ديـ ـيني   ـون   بـ ـ
ديـو   ديـ   ميـ   طيـ ـ مِـ   وَيـ   يَمَـ
بـا   ـها   ـ لا   ـ زَما   لُبـ ا   لُبـ ا ـي
هـا ـي   بِدوـي   يَمَـ ـي   لِأَـي   يابا ـي   يابا   ألاَـ
آ ـ   أَلْأَوا ـ   آذا ـ   ـار   ـور   إ ـ   ـمور   ـمـ ـم
نيرا ـ   ـام   أَـا   آـي   آذا ـي   إذْـي   إـي
لَيْمو ـ   مَمْنو ـ   مَمْـ ونَة   ليـ ـا   هُـ ا   دِيـ ا   دِينَـ ا
ديـ هُم   ـائل   ـائي   أريزوـ ا   ـايروبي   تايْوا ـ
هـ ـد   هِـ ـدي   هِ ـدِيَة   طَنْزاـ يَة   أورلاـ دو   أطْلاـ طَة
ـهار   لُبْناـ يَة   أـ ا   أـ ا إيراـ يَة   أـ ا هِـ ديَة   أنا
يَمَـ يَة   أَلْأُرْدُ ـ   مـ ـن   بدو ـ   بَـ طَلون   لِأَـ ـه
مِليوـ ير   ـادي   لَـ ـدَن   أهْلاً   هِـ ري   نيـ ـا
لِلاَـ   ـهاد   ـهر أَلْنيل   هُـ ا   طَـ   ـور   تَـور
إ ـ

89

Chapter 5 — jeem: جيم   j: ج

This Arabic letter name is jeem: جيم and it sounds like the English "j" as in "just". The jeem: جيم is a consonant and it is given the symbol "j" in this book, as in (George: joorj جورج). The jeem is also used to represent the "ch" sound as in (chips: جِبْس). The جيم has four shapes: beginning ‍جـ, middle ‍ـجـ, end ـج, and isolated ج:

ج	ـج	ـجـ	جـ
زوج	إنْج	زِنْجي	جيب

❶ Read these Arabic words aloud slowly focusing on the four shapes of jeem: جيم:

George:	جورج	jeem:	جيم
very (f):	جداً	good (f):	جَيد
glass:	زُجاج	jell-O:	جَلي
my chickens:	دِجاجي	chickens:	دِجاج
poultry:	دواجِن	a chicken ♀:	دِجاجَة
inch:	إنْج	skull:	جُمْجُمَة
beautiful:	جَميل	beauty/male name:	جَمال
attractive:	جَذاب	face:	وَجْه
husband/pair:	زَوْج	star:	نَجْم
wife:	زَوْجَة	my husband:	زَوْجي
my marriage:	زَواجي	marriage:	زَواج
heaven:	جَنَة	hell:	جَهَنَم
new ♀:	جَديدة	new:	جَديد
crazy ♀:	مَجْنَزنَة	crazy:	مَجْنون
murderer ♀:	مُجْرِمَة	murderer:	مُجْرِم
persistent (pl):	مُجاهِدَة	persistent:	مُجاهِد
Tigress River:	نَهْر دِجْلَة	river:	نَهْر
he brings:	يَجيب	must:	يَجِب
I bring:	أجيب	bring:	جيب
they bring:	يَجيبون	we bring:	نَجيب

African race: زِنْج		Azerbaijan: أَذَرْبِيجان	
African male: زِنْجِي		African people: زِنوج	
Algeria: أَلْجَزائِر		African ♀: زِنْجِية	
The Republic of Algeria: أَلْجِمْهورِيَة أَلْجَزائِرِيَة			

❷ Read aloud the جيم with other learned letters, five times per page:

جا   جا   جاجا   جو   جو   جوجو   جيجيي   راجي

جيجو   بيجو   جيج   جيجاج   ديج   ذيج   هيج   جيجوج

جيجيج   بوجيج   باجيج   جاجيج   لاج   هاج   جاجوج

جاجاج   لاجوج   جالاج   لاجاج   جيلاج   لاجِئ   باجي

جورج   موج   لوج   دوج   داج   زاج   آج   أَجأَج   آجي

أَجي   جاج   جَج   جوج   جُج   جيج   جِج   طَج   جِج

جِجج   بَجاج   لَجوج   زُجاج   رَجرَج   زَج   لَج   جورج

جَميل.   جورج جَذّاب.   جَمال جَميل.   جورج

جَميل جِداً.   جورج جَذّاب جِداً.   جَمال جَميل جِداً.   جَمال رَجُل

جَذّاب جِداً.   جيب دِجاج.   جيب زُجاج.   جَيِّد جِداً.   جيب دِجاج

جَيِّد.   جيب جَلي جَيِّد جِداً.   جيب دِجاج جَيِّد جِداً.   دِجاجي جَيِّد.

دِجاجي جَيِّد جِداً.   جَديد   دِجاجي جَديد.   دِجاجي جَديد وَلَذيذ جِداً.

زَوْجي جَيِّد جِداً.   زَوْجي مُجاهِد جِداً.   زَوْجي جَميل.   زَوْجي

زَوْج	جَمال زَوْج لَيْلى.	زَوْجي نَجم.	زَوْجي زِنْجي.	جَذاب.
زَوْج لَيْلى جَذاب وَجَميل وَمُجاهِد وَجَيِد جِداً.		زَواجي مِن زَوْجي جَيِد جِداً.		
وَجْه	لَيْلى جَذابة.	لَيْلى جَميلَة.	زَواج لَيْلى جَيِد.	
جَمال يَجيب	جورْج يَجيب دِجاج.	لَيْلى زَوْجة جَيِدَة.	لَيْلى جَميل.	
هُوَ يَجيب	جَمال يَجيب دِجاجَة.	زَوْجي يَجيب دِجاج.	دِجاج.	
هُوَ يَجيب دِجاجَة	جَمال يَجيب دِجاجَة.	دِجاجَة وأَنا أَجيب دِجاجَة.		
وأَنا أَجيب دِجاجَة.	جَمال يَجيب دِجاجَة.	هُوَ يَجيب دِجاجَة وأَنا		
يَجِب أَنْ أَزور نَهَر دِجْلَة.	يَجِب أَنْ أَزور اَلْجَزائِر	أَجيب دِجاجَة.		
وَطَن جَميلَة.	لا يَجِب أَنْ أَزور أَذَرْبيجان.	يَجِب أَنْ أَزور وَطَني		
يَجِب أَنْ أَزور أُمي دائِما.	يَجِب أَنْ أَزور لَيْلى وَجَمال.	أَوْلاً.		

❸ Practice writing these four shapes of the letter جيم:

ج ـج ـجـ جـ

ج ـج ـجـ جـ
زَوج إِنْج زِنْجي جيب

←

جا جـ جـ جـ نَجد جـ جـ جـ

إنْج ـجـ ـجـ ـجـ جورج ج ج ج

جا جاجا جو جوجو جي جيجي راجي ماجي

جيجو بيجو جيجاج جيجج ديج ذيج هيج

جيج جيجوج بوجيج باجيج جاجيج لاج هاج

جاجوج جاجاج لاجوج جالاج لاجاج جيلاج

لاجئ باجي جورج موج لوج دوج داج زاج

آج إج آجي جاج جَج جُج جوج جج جيج

93

جورج	ججوج	ججاج	ججيج	ججج	جج
دِجاجي	دِجاج	إنْج	جَلي	زُجاج	جَيد جِداً	جيم
وَجْه	جَذاب	جَميل	جَماء	جُمْجُمَة	دَواجِن	دِجاجَة
جَنَة	نَجْم	زَواجي	زَوْجَتي	زَوْجَة	زَوْج	زَواج
مُجاهِد	مُجرِمَة	مُجرِم	مَجنونَة	مَجنون	جَهَنَم
نَجيب	يُجيب	أُجيب	يَجِب	نَهَر دِجْلَة	مُجاهِدين
زِنْجي	زنوج	زِنْج	أذرْبَيجان	يُجاوب	يُجيبون
جَديد	ألْجُمهوريَة ألْجَزائِريَة	ألْجَزائِر	زِنْجيَة

❹ Pick the correct shape of the letter جيم to fill in these blanks:

ج   ج   جـ   جـ
ج   ـجـ   ـجـ   ـج

را_ي   جي_ي   _ي   _و_و   _ا_ا   _و   _ا
_ذي   _جي   ما_ي   _يجو   جي_اج   جيلا   نا_ي
جيجو   بو_يج   جيجي   _ا_ا   _هَدي_   هي_
جا_وج   جا_اج   _لا   جاجي   با_يج   ها
_جُ   _جَ   جا_   با_ي   لا_ئ   جالا   لا_وج
_زا   _دا   _دو   _لو   مو_   جور   _جِ
أ_يب   _جي   _جِ   _جو   _آ_ي   _أ_   آ_
زوا_   زُ_اج   يَ_يبون   نَ_يب   جج   يَ_يب
دوا_ن   دِ_اجي   دِ_ا_ة   دِ_اج   وَ_ه   زوا_ي
_هِنَم   _نَة   _ذاب   يُ_اوب   _دا_   يِّد   يَ_ب
جـ_ـوج   ججبا   ججيي   دجلة   رَ_اء   _اء
بنـ_   إنـ_ة   زَوـ_ة   أَذَرْبَيـ_ان   زِنـ_ي   نَـ_م   _مال
_مال _ذاب.   _مال _ميل.   جورْ _ذاب.   _ورْج _ميل.
_ورج وَ _مال _ميلان.   _مال _ميل _داً.   _ورج _ميل _داً.

Chapter 6   س: s   سين :seen

This Arabic letter name is seen سين and it sounds like the English "s" as in "simple." The seen سين is a consonant and it is given the symbol "s" in this book, as in (CD: see dee سي دي). The سين has four shapes: beginning ـسـ, middle ـسـ, end ـس, and isolated س. Do not write yet; first see the four shapes of سين alone and in words:

س	ـس	ـسـ	سـ
ناس	باريس	نيسان	سين

❶ Learning Step One: Read these words aloud and focus on the four shapes of سين:

seen:	سين	cinema ♀:	سينَما
sandwich:	سَنْدَويج	CD:	سي دي
Saturday:	سَبْت	fat:	سمين
Paris:	باريس	Asia:	آسْيَة
Russia:	روسيَة	penicillin:	بَنْسَلين
soup:	سوب	sesame:	سِمسِم
peace:	سلام	the peace:	أَلسَلام
the safety ♀:	أَلسَلامَة	Sudan:	سودان
name:	إِسْم	my name:	إِسْمي
evening:	مَساء	letter:	رِسالَة
prison:	سِجْن	easy:	سَهْل
brunette:	أَسْمَر	brunette ♀:	سَمْرة
question:	سؤال	ask:	إِسْأَل
I ask:	أَنا أَسْأَل	not yet:	لِسه لا
sky:	سَماء	Tripoli:	طَرابلُس
year ♀:	سَنَة	school ♀:	مَدْرَسَة
black:	أَسْوَد	car ♀:	سَيّارَة
diamonds:	أَلْماس	stepped on:	داس
head:	راس	people:	ناس
human:	إِنْسان	April:	نيسان

The Arabic Alphabet for English Speakers

massage:	مِساج	responsible:	مَسْؤول
mosque:	مَسْجِد	tooth:	سِن
kiss (v.):	بوس	only/enough:	بَس
next to:	جَنب	compromise (v.):	ساوم

❷ Read aloud the سين with other learned letters; read five times per page: ←

سا ساسا سو سوسو سي سيسي راسي لاسي

واسي مآسي سيسو داسوا سيس بوسيس

موس دوس بوس روس زوس جوس جاسوس

سيبيس سيسيس وسويس سوسوس سيسوس ساساس

سايس سِياسي داس ناس لاس راس راسي آسْيَا

سيلان سيسيلْيَة سِنونو باريس لوس أَنْجِلُس سينَما

سوب سي دي سي آي أي سَنْدَويج بْروس بَطاطِس

سين سِن سَمين سَبْت سَنَة سيب يُساوِم

سَهم سائِل ساس سَس سُس سوس سيس سِس

إسْمي سيمون. أنا من لوس أَنْجِلُس. أَريد سَنْدَويج رِجاءً. أَريد

أَسأل سؤال. وَين أَلْسينَما؟ وَين أَلْمَدْرَسَة؟ وَين أَلْسِجْن؟ وَين

أَلْمَسؤول؟ وَين أَلْناس؟. وَين أَلْمَسْجِد أَلْجَديد؟ لازِم آخُذ

بَنْسَلين أَلْآن. أَريد سوب أَلْآن. أَريد سَنْدَويج أَلْآن. أَلْزَمان أَلْآن

أَلسَّيَّارَة جَديدَة	أَلسَّنَة هِيَ سَنَة ٢٠٢٣	هو نيسان ٢٠٢٣
أَلسَّيَّارَة سودَة.	أَلسَّيَّارَة هِيَ سَيَّارَة جَمال.	موديل ٢٠٢٣.
جَمال يُريد سَيَّارَة جَديدَة.	جَمال أَسْمَر أَلْلون.	لَيلى سَمْرَة وَجَميلَة.
هُوَ يَريد	جَمال إِنْسان وَطَني.	لَيلى تُريد سي دي جَديد وَبَس.
إِلسّلامَة وبَس.	جَمال يُريد يِسْأل لَيلى سؤال	وَهُوَ لا يريد أَلْماس.
مُهِمّ.	جاءَ جَمال لَيْلَة رأس إِلسَّنَة.	جَمال زار طَرابْلُس وَباريس،
لازم	أَريد أَزور روسْيَة.	أَلرِسالَة جَنْب أَلطّاوْلَة. وَزار آسيا.
أَريد	أَريد أَسأل سؤال سَهْل.	أَزور جِنوب أَلسّودان وَأَزور سورْيا.
سَلام وبَس.	وَيْن هِيَ؟ وَيْن أَرْسِل جواب بِالْبَريد؟	وَيْن أَلْمَطار؟
	وَيْن أَلمَدينَة أَلْجَديدَة؟	وَيْن أَلنادي؟

❸ Learning Step Three: Practice writing the four shapes of the letter سين:

ماسي	راسي	سيسي	سي	سوسو	سو	ساسا	سا

ما سي   راسي   سيسي   سي   سوسو   سو   ساسا   سا

زُس   إس   دِس   دَس   سَم   سي   سو   سا

لوس أنْجِلِس   سِمسِم   سينَما   سودان   بْروس   سين

سيسو   لاسي   راسي   سيسي   سوسو   ساسا

راسي   داس   سِياسي   سايس   سيسيس   دوس   سيس

سيب   سوب   باريس   سِنْسِنادي   سيسيلْيَة   سيلان   آسْيَا

سَمين   سِني   سن   سَنْدَويج   سي آي أي   سي دي   ساب

بَس   لِسَه   أسْمَر   إسْمي   إسْم   سائِل   سَهْم   سَنة   سَبت

ألسَّلامَة   سَلام   سِس   سيس   سُس   سوس   سَس   ساس

		Part Three
Chapter 7	21-100	Numbers أرقام

Read these 21-100 Arabic numbers from right to left←. Read the number 21 starting with the one first and then the 20. Consequently, 21 would be (one and twenty واحِد وعِشرون). The numbers in this book are presented in the formal Arabic dialect (FuSHaw فُصحى):

21:	waa'·Hid we·Aish·roon'	واحِد وعِشرون	٢١
22:	'ith·neen' weAishroon	إثْنَين وعِشرون	٢٢
23:	the·laa'·thah weAishroon	ثَلاثَة وعِشرون	٢٣
24:	'er'·be·Aeh weAishroon	أرْبَعة وعِشرون	٢٤
25:	khem'·seh weAishroon	خَمسَة وعِشرون	٢٥
26:	si'·teh weAishroon	سِتَة وعِشرون	٢٦
27:	seb'·Aeh weAishroon	سَبْعَة وعِشرون	٢٧
28:	the·maan'·yeh weAishroon	ثَمانْيَة وعِشرون	٢٨
29:	tis'·Aeh weAishroon	تِسْعَة وعِشرون	٢٩
30:	the·laa·thoon'	ثَلاثون	٣٠
31:	waa'·Hid we·the·laa·thoon'	واحِد وثَلاثون	٣١
32:	'ithneen wethelaathoon	إثْنَين وثَلاثون	٣٢
39:	tisAeh wethelaathoon	تِسْعَة وثَلاثون	٣٣
40:	'er·be·Aoon'	أرْبَعون	٤٠
41:	waa'·Hid we'er·be·Aoon'	واحِد وأرْبَعون	٤١
49:	tis'·Aeh we'er·be·Aoon'	تِسْعَة وأرْبَعون	٤٩
50:	khem·soon'	خمسون	٥٠
51:	waa'·Hid we·khem·soon'	واحِد وخَمْسون	٥١
60:	si·toon'	سِتون	٦٠
70:	seb·Aoon'	سَبْعون	٧٠
80:	the·maa·noon'	ثَمانون	٨٠
90:	tis·Aoon'	تِسْعون	٩٠
100:	mi·'eh/mi·'yeh	مِئَة or مِيَه	١٠٠
100:	maa'eh/ maa'et	مائه / مائة	١٠٠

REVIEW

Chart of the Six Learned Letters in Part Three and their Shapes

باء :b				
ب	بـ	ـبـ	ـب	بـ
روب	طِب	طِبي	باء	

ميم :m				
م	م	ـمـ	مـ	
آدَم	أَلَم	دائِما	ميل	

هاء :h				
ه	ـه	ـهـ	هـ	
أبوه	أمُه	مُهم	هي	

نون :n				
ن	ن	ـنـ	نـ	
نون	طَن	هُنا	نور	

جيم :j				
ج	ـج	ـجـ	جـ	
زَوج	إنج	زِنْجي	جيب	

سين :s				
س	ـس	ـسـ	سـ	
ناس	باريس	نيسان	سين	

Summary of the Arabic Vowels and Six other Symbols

da: دَ   daa: دا   du: دُ   doo: دو

di: دِ   dee: دي   -dan: دً   dd: دّ

dl: دْل   aw: ى   ă=aa: آ   ': ء

Practice Test of the Learned Letters

ا و د ذ ر ز ط ي ل   ب م هـ ن ج س

Translate these sounds and words into Arabic letters:

seen	jeem	haa'	meem	baa'

saamee	baab	blooz	boodheh	buTul

Taalib	ribaaT	beT	zeebreh	beraazeel

baawdir	soob	beebee	baarood	roobert

Tebeeb	bidoon	maamaa	mooz	medreed

roomeh	maalee	laam	moodeyl	mey

meTaar	miraayaa	memTooT	'um	'ew

lemmaa	'ekl	benseleen	'umee	sukker

seyyaareh	ădem	sooăl	'alăn	shukren

daa'imen	haa'	hemzeh	behaar	muhim

hedher	'oohaayoo	werdeh	muhimeh	meddeh

zelaaTeh	TemaaTim	beTaaTeh	maalTeh	'ezmeh

hiye	huwe	hedhaa	yelleh	dheheb

'eyweh	lehaa	'eboohaa	'umehaa	he'ulaa'

naanaa	bidoon	leymoon	taaywaan	jemeel

weyn	'ereezoonaa	meen	milyooneyyer	yemen

naar	'enaa	benTeloon	Tenzaanyeh	'eTlaanTeh

lendaa	min	'el'urdun	flaawenzeh	'elaan

lenden	naayroobee	lilaan	li*aa*'enehu	jeem

joorj	mejnoon	jiden	dijaaj	jelee

jemaal	zewj	zinj	'edharbeyjaan	nejm

zewjeh	jumjumeh	mujrim	'inj	mij

mujaahid	mujaahideen	'eljazaa'ir	jumhooriyeh	'eljimhooriyeh

'eljezaa'iriyeh	broos	soodaan	seenemaa	simsim

sendeweej	see dee	see aay 'ey	loos 'enjulus	baarees

liseh laa	roosyeh	ăsyaa	benseleen	soob

selaam	'el selaam	'el selaameh	'ism	'ismee

'isaa'el	sooăl	mesoo'ool	'insaan	seneh

'esmer	semreh	sehl	medreseh	semaa'

memnoon	haadhaa	mesjid	'el'ezher	'eswed

PART FOUR
Seven More Letters

Name	Symbol	As in	Isolated	End	Middle	Beginning
taa': تاء	t	tip	ت	ـت	ـتـ	تـ
faa': فاء	f	fill	ف	ـف	ـفـ	فـ
kaaf: كاف	k	kit	ك	ـك	ـكـ	كـ
Daad: ضاد	D	eggs: beyD	ض	ـض	ـضـ	ضـ
Aeyn: عَين	A	Arabic	ع	ـع	ـعـ	عـ
sheen: شين	sh	ship	ش	ـش	ـشـ	شـ
Haa': حاء	H	Love: Hub	ح	ـح	ـحـ	حـ

Isolated	End	Middle	Behinning
ت	ـت	ـتـ	تـ
ف	ـف	ـفـ	فـ
ك	ـك	ـكـ	كـ
ض	ـض	ـضـ	ضـ
ع	ـع	ـعـ	عـ
ش	ـش	ـشـ	شـ
ح	ـح	ـحـ	حـ

Chapter 1 — ت t: — تاء taa':

This Arabic letter name is taa' تاء and it sounds like the English "t" as in "tip". The letter taa' تاء is a consonant and it is given the symbol "t" in this book as in (tennis: te'·nes تَنَس). The تاء has four shapes: beginning تـ, middle ـتـ, end ـت, and isolated ت. Do not write yet; first see the four shapes of تاء in words:

ت   ـت   ـتـ   تـ

تاء   زَيْتون   تِوالَيت   بَيْروت

❶ Read these Arabic words aloud slowly focusing on the four shapes of taa' تاء.

taa':	تاء	Detroit:	ديتْرويْت
Cincinnati:	سِنْسِناتي	Tunisia:	تونِس
Taiwan:	تايْوان	Trinidad:	تِرْنْداد
Thailand:	تايْلانْد	Budapest:	بوداپَسْت
Beirut:	بَيْروت	Robert:	روبَرت
tennis:	تَنَس	toilet:	تِوالَيت
Hitler:	هِتْلَر	death:	مَوت
house:	بَيْت	figs:	تين
daughter/girl:	بِنْت	girls:	بَنات
plants:	نَباتات	when (f):	مَتى
husband:	زَوْج	wife:	زَوْجَة
excellent:	مُمْتاز	olives:	زَيتون
olive oil:	زَيْت ألزَيتون	conference:	مؤتَمَر
you:	إَنْتَ	you ♀:	إَنْتِ
bring:	جيب	I bring:	أنا أجيب
he brings:	هُوَ يَجيب	she brings:	هي تَجيب
you bring:	إِنْتَ تَجيب	you bring ♀:	إِنْتِ تَجيبِ
we bring:	نَحْنُ نَجيب	they bring:	هُم يَجيبون
car:	سَيّارَة	school:	مَدْرَسَة

❷ Read the taa' تاء with other learned letters aloud five times per page:

تيت	تيتي	تي	توتو	تو	تو	تاتا	تا	تَأْ	←
هيت	زَيْت	تات	مات	بات	ذات	هات	آت	آيات	بَيْت
تيتات	بوت	موت	توت	زيتي	هاتي	ذاتي			آتي
تاتيت	باتيت	بوتات	بوتيت		تيتت			توتوت	
تاتات	تاء مَرْبوطَة	آت	تالات	لاتوت	تاتات		تاتوت		
تونس	تَنَس	تَبولي	تَمام	إِنْتِ	إِنْتَ	آهات	تَمْر		تَنْوين
جابت	تَجيب	نامَت	تَنام	تَهْرَب	رِتْبَتُه	يَتيم			مَيِّت
وَدِرَت	تِدْري		رادَت تَموت وَماتَت.	تَريد	طارَت			تَطير	
إِهْتِمام	طَلَبَت	تِطْلُب	دِرِسِت	تِدْرُس	جاءَت				وتجي
سِنْسِناتي	تونس	تايوان	ديترويت	بَيْروت	إِهْتَمَت				تِهْتَم
تَطْوير	تَتات	تِثْت	تِتِ	تيتي	تُثْ	تَتوت	تَت		ناتا
مُتَطَوِر	مُرْتَبِط	مُرْتَبِطَة	مَرْبوط	مَرْبوطَة	تاء مَرْبوطَة				
مَدينة	سَيّارَة	مَدْرِسَة	تَم	لَم يَتِم	يَتوب	يُطيل	يَتْلو		
يُتَمْتِم									

taa' mer·boo'·Teh (ة ـة) تاء مَرْبوطَة

The meaning of the word "of" is expressed in a special type of "t" called (taa' mer·boo'·Teh تاء مَرْبوطَة). If a word that ends with eh, as in (car: sey·yaa'·reh سَيّارَة) is followed by "of" or a possessor (an owner), that end "h" changes to a "t." Ex., car: sey·yaa'·reh سَيّارَة followed by Sam become →the car of Sam (Sam's car): (sey·yaa'·ret saam سَيّارَة سام). Because this type of a final "t" is originated from a final "h," it looks like a final "h" but with two dots above it like this (ة ـة). The written version of this is always with a "t" regardless of how it's pronounced. Read examples of the end "h" sounding like "t" when followed by an "of" or a possessor:

sey·yaa'·reh سَيّارَه →seyyaaret Sam   سَيّارَة سام

med'·re·seh: school مَدْرِسَه →medreset Sam   مَدْرِسَة سام

be·Taa'·Teh بَطاطَه →beTaaet Leylaw   بطاطَة لَيلى

sey·yaa'·reh سَيّارَه →sey·yaa·'ret 'elbint   سَيّارَة ألْبِنْت

me·dee·'neh مَدينَه →me·dee·'net Saam   مَدينَة سام

Republic of Algeria: جِمْهورَية ألْجَزائِر

the school of the student: مَدْرِسَة ألْطالِب

the language of Japan/Japan's language: لُغَة ألْيابان

a little bit of water: shwey'·yet mey   شْوَيَة مَي

The Arabic Alphabet for English Speakers

❸ Practice writing the four shapes of تاء and the two shapes of تاء مَرْبوطَة:

تـ ـتـ ـت ت
تاء زيتون بنت ذات ـة

تـ ـتـ ـت ت
تاء زيتون بنت ذات ـة

←

مَتى	ـتـ ـتـ ـتـ ـتـ	تـ ـتـ ـت تاء
ذات	ت ت ت ت	ـت ـت ـت ـت بت
تيتي	ذاب	تي	تيتو	تاتو	توتو	تاتا	تي	تو	تا
ذات	بات	مات	تات	زيت	بيت	هيت	تيت
زيتي	هاتي	ذاتي	آتي	آت	آيات	هات
بوتيت	تيتت	توتوت	تيتوت	بوت	موت	توت
تمام	تم	تبن	تمر	تين	تَنْوين	تاء مَرْبوطَة
آهات	رتبتُه	يتيم	ميت	تونس	تنس	تبولي

109

نامَت	جابَت	طارَت	تَطير	تُريد	رادت	تموت

ماتت	تِدري	دِرت	تجي	جاءَت	تِدْرُس	تِهتَم

دِرسَت	تِطلب	طِلبت	إهْتَمَت	بِبَيروت	ديتْرويت

بِتونِس	تَنَس	تاتا	تَتَ	توتو	تُتُ	تيتي	تِتِ

روبرت	هِتلر	بَيت	بنت	بَنات	نَباتات	ولادات

تَمام	تمر	تِمور	تَموز	تَنورة	زَيت ألْزيتون	مَتى

مُؤتَمر	مُمتاز	بنت	ألْبنت	ولايات	بيوت	نَباتات

إنتَ	إنتِ	سَيّارة سام	مَدْرَسة سام	بطاطة لَيلى	سَيّارة ألْبنت

مَدينَة ليلى	جمْهورَية ألْجَزائِر	لُغَة ألْيابان	شوَيَة ليمون

The Arabic Alphabet for English Speakers

❹ Pick the correct shape of the letter تاء and تاء مَرْبوطَة to fill in these blanks. Keep in mind that the تاء
مَرْبوطَة that sounds like a "t" is always followed by another word (usually a possessor):

←

_ا_ا _و_و _يتو _ي تي_ي ما_ ها _ آ

آيا_ بي_ زي_ آ_ي ذا_ي زي_ي تو_

مو_ _ابو_ لاهو_ _نوين _مر _مام آها_

_اء مَرْبوطَ _نْوين إن_ _ إن_ _مَيِّ _بْولي

_نَس _ونِس يَ_يم رِتبَ_ـه _نام نام_ _جيب

جاب_ _طير طار _ريد راد _موت ما_ت

دري در _جي جاء _طلب _ إهْ_مَت

بَيرو_ دي_رويت _رنداد سنسانا _ايوان _ايلاند

بودابس_ روبر_ ه_لر توالي_ مو_ م_ى

بي_ بيو_ بن_ بنا_ با_ نبا_ا_ ولادا

_مر _مور _موز _نورة زي_ أَلْزي_ون مُؤْ_مر

مُمـ_از سَيّارَ_ سام مَدْرسَ_ سام بطاطَ_ لَيلى سَيّارَة أَلْبِنْ_

مَدينَ_ ليلى جِمْهورَيَ_ أَلْجَزائِر _ا_ا _و_و _ي_ي

لُغَ_ أَليابان شْوَيَ_ ليمون _مـ_ _مادي ي_مادى

تـ_مادى _تورط _ طاول

111

Chapter 2	f: ف	faa': فاء

This Arabic letter name is faa' فاء and it sounds like the English "f" as in "fill". The letter فاء is a consonant and it is given the symbol "f" in this book as in (film: فِلْم). Notice that Arabic doesn't have a letter equivalent to the English "v" as in television, oven, etc. However, Arabic speakers may say the "v" in oven and write 'ōo·fin أوفِن with an "f." The فاء has four shapes: beginning فـ, middle ـفـ, final ـف, and isolated ف:

ف   ـف   ـفـ   فـ

رف   لطيف   تلفون   في

❶ Read these Arabic words aloud slowly focusing on the four shapes of faa' فاء:

television:	تَلَفِزْيون	telephone:	تَلِفون
oven:	أوفِن	office:	أوفيس
Orlando:	أورْلانْدو	Sudan:	سودان
Tunisia:	تونِس	Palestine:	فَلَسْطين
Venezuela:	فَنْزويلا	furnace:	فِرْنِس
Philippine:	فيلِبين	Memphis:	مَمْفَس
philosophy:	فَلْسَفَة	Plato:	أَفْلاطون
file:	فايَل	vitamin:	فيتامين
7-up:	سَفِن أَب	France:	فَرَنْسا
millionaire:	مِلْيونير	physics:	فيزْياء
influenza:	فْلاوَنْزَة	'e·lif:	أَلِف
fava-beans:	فول	falafel:	فَلافِل
pepper:	فِلْفِل	there is/in:	في
shelf:	رَف	synonym:	مُرادِف
money:	فْلوس	travel:	سافِر
from:	مِن	from the:	مْنِل
art:	فَنّ	arts:	فنون
artist:	فَنان	educated:	دارِس
human being:	إنْسان	humanist:	إنْساني
because:	لِأَنَه	purple:	بَنَفْسِجي

so and so:	فُلان	breakfast:	فِطور
notebook:	دَفْتَر	stove:	فُرن
wrap:	لَف	nice:	لَطيف
six: ٦	سِتَة	merciful:	رَؤوف
April:	نيسان	March:	آذار
July:	تَموز	May:	أيار
September:	أيلول	August:	آب

❷ Read the faa' فاء with other learned letters aloud five times per page: ←

ريفي فيفي في فيفو فو فوفو فافا فَا

فيفوف طوف دَف لِف فافيف بافيف بوفيف

فافاف فيفاف فافوف لافوف لوف بوفوف فوفوف

لَفِلف لِف زِف هِتاف جَفاف زَفاف آلاف فالاف

فُطير فَريد أَنْفُه فَراوْلَة فِاف فَف فاء أَنْف آفات

طَفيف فيل رفوفُه رفوف رَف فَي لَطيف طَريف

فَنِهايَة فِلْم ذَرَف مُرادِف جايِف فَيَجِب طايِف هَف

فِف فُف فَف فَطَلَبت فَطَلَب فَفَهَم فَدِرَسَ إِهْتِف

بِنَفْسِه فَتاجَرَ

The Arabic Alphabet for English Speakers

❸ Practice writing these four shapes of the letter فاء:

ف ف ف ف

ف ف ف ف

فاء تلفون لَطيف رَف

فاء ف ف ف ف   ف ف ف ف في

لِف ف ف ف ف   رَف ف ف ف ف

فا فو في فافا فوفو فافو فيتو فايل فَنّ

فيف ريف بافيف بوفيف فافيت زيف دَف

ففف طوف فيفوف بوفوف فافوف

لافوف فوفو ففاف فُفُ فيفي فِفِ فافا فَفَ

تَلَفون تَلَفِزْيون جَفْتُ فَم فاهُهُ فَل مَفْتول مَفْهوم

أوفيس أوفِن فِنْزويلا طَنزانْية أريزونَة فَلَسْطين

مَمْفَس فيلِبّين فيِتْنام فَرَنْسا فايل فِرْنس أَلِف

114

فُلُوس	دَفْتَر	فَلْسَفَة	أَفْلاطون	فيزْياء	فْلاوَنْزَة

رَؤُف	فَنّان	فِنون	فَنّ	فَلافِل	فِلْفِل	سافِر

لَفيف	فُفّ	فوفو	بَنَفْسَجي	فِطور	فُلان	فُرْن

❹ Pick the correct shape of the letter فاء to fill in these blanks:

ف ف ف ف

رَف   لَطيف   تلفون   فاء

←

_ا_ا_ _و_و _يفو _ي_ في_ي ري_ي ري_ _في

بافي_ بو_يف فافي_ _زي_ _ل_ طو_ _د_

فيفو لاو_وف _افوف فَ_ _فُ_ _فِ_

في_ي تل_زيون تل_ون أو_يس _ف _ _ ف _ اف

أو_ن _رْن _لَسْطين _نزويلا _رنس _يل _ي

ممـ_ـس _يلبين _يتنام _رنسا _اهم _يزياء

أ_لاطون فلسـ_ـة دَ_تر سـ_ـر _لوس مـ_ـلس فل_ل

فلا_ل _ن _نان _نون رَؤ_ _لان _طور

بن_سجي _تى مـ_ـتي مَلْهو_ تـ_ـسير هتـ_

_سَيْ

Chapter 3 — ك k: — كاف kaaf

This Arabic letter name is kaaf كاف and it sounds like the English "k" as in "kiss". The letter كاف is a consonant and it is given the symbol "k" in this book as in (camera: kaa'·mi'·reh كَامِرَة). The كاف has four shapes: beginning كـ, middle ـكـ, final ـك, and isolated ك.

ك   ـك   ـكـ   كـ

دانيمارْك   سَمَك   أَمْريكَا   كاف

❶ Read these Arabic words aloud slowly focusing on the four shapes of kaaf كاف:

Oklahoma:	أوكْلاهومَة	Nicaragua:	نيكاراكْوَة
doctor:	دِكتور	doctor ♀:	دِكْتورَة
Ph.D.:	دِكْتوراه	but: laa'·kin	لَكِن
kilo:	كيلو	kilowatt:	كيلوواط
kaaf:	كاف	kes'·reh:	كَسْرَة
si·koon':	سِكون	dog:	كَلْب
he wanted you to:	أرادَك	this: haa'·dhaa	هَذا
like/as: prefix ke-	كَـ	like this:	كَهَذا
like that:	كَهَذاك	like Raazee:	كَرازي
like the bank:	كَألْبَنْك	cake:	كيك
chemistry:	كيمْياء	hammer:	جاكوج
sugar:	سُكَّر	smart:	ذَكي
good:	كُوَّيِس	Kuwait:	كِوَيت
eat:	كُل	I eat:	أنا آكُل
book:	كِتاب	my: suffix ee	ي or ـي
my book:	كِتابي	fish:	سَمَك
my fish:	سَمَكي	request (n.):	طَلَب
my order:	طَلَبي	my dog:	كَلْبي
your: suffix -ek	ـك	your book:	كِتابَك
your order:	طَلَبَك	your dog:	كَلْبَك

like my dog:	كَكَلْبي	like your dog:	كَكَلْبَك
lesson:	دَرْس	your lesson:	دَرْسَك
my food:	أَكْل	your food:	أَكْلَك
Mexico:	مَكْسيك	Mexican:	مَكْسيكي
America:	أَمْريكًا	American:	أَمْريكي
English:	إِنْكِليزي	The English language (f):	اَلإِنْكِليزِيَة
was:	كان	microphone:	مايْكروفون

The Arabic Alphabet for English Speakers

❷ Read aloud the kaaf كاف with other learned letters five times per page:

هَيك هاك ذاك كافْكا كيكي كي كيكو كوكو كو كا

كَيْكَة كَيك كَرْكوك كوك زَكي هاكي زَيك بَيَك

باكيك كاكيك بوكيك كيكك كوكوك كيكاك

لَكَ لَكُم تِكْتاك مَكوك كالاك لاكوك كاكوك كاكاك

كُل يَتَكَهَّن كفى فِكْرَة تَكْلِفَة جوكَر زَجَك دَك

جابَك رَكَب كَنَسَ كَكَريم كَريم كَهَذاك كَهذا هَجاك

لاس فيكَس ألاسْكا أوكْلاهوما طَلَبَك دَرْسِك رادَك

كامِرَة أمْريكِيَة أمْريكي نيكاراكوِة دَنيمارْك

دِكْتورَة دِكْتور كيلوْواط آلِكْس ذَكي كْلاسيكي كارْتون

كوبَهُ كوب كيمْياء بْلاسْتيك كَسْرة سِكون دِكْتوراه

أتَكيت أنا آكُل كُل أكُل كُوَيْت كُوَّيِس سُكَّر كوبَها

مَكْسيك كيتو أكْوادور راديكالي كِتابَك كِتابي كِتاب

لَكِن مَكْدوس كَج أب هَمْبَرْكِر سَمَك كَباب بَنْك كَلْب

إلَيْكِ لِكِ يَكْ كُ أُمَكَ لَكَ كُرْكُم دينَك بَكى

The Arabic Alphabet for English Speakers

❸ Practice writing these four shapes of the letter كاف:

ك ـك ـكـ كـ

ك ـك ـكـ كـ

ذاك سمك لكن كاف

كـ كـ كـ كـ كاف   ـكـ ـكـ ـكـ ـكـ   مَكَّة

ـك ـك ـك ـك أَك   ك ك ك ك   هاك

كا كو كي كاكي كوكو كيك ذاك هاك دَك

كا كو كوكو كي كيكي كافْكا هَيك بَيك

إِزَيك هاكي زَكي كوك كَرْكوك كَيك كَيْكَة كيكاك

كيكوك كوكوك كيكك بوكيك كاكيك باكيك كاكاك

كاكوك لاكوك كالاك مَكوك تِكْتاك لَكُم لَكَ

دَك زَجَك جوكَر تَكْلِفَة فِكْرَة كفى بَتَكَهَن كُل

119

The Arabic Alphabet for English Speakers

هَجاك	كَهذا	كَهَذاك	كَريم	كَكَريم	كَنسَ	رَكَبَ
جابَك	رادَك	دَرسِك	طَلَبَك	أوكْلاهوما		لاس فيكَس
ألاسْكا	دَنيمارْك	نيكاراكوة	أمْريكِة	أمْريكي		أمْريكِية
كامِرَة	كارْتون	كْلاسيكي	ذَكي	آلِكْس		كيلوْواط
دِكْتور	دِكْتورَة	دِكْتوراه	سِكون	كَسْرة		بْلاسْتيك
كيمْياء	كوب	كوبَهُ	كوبَها	سُكَّر	كُوَّيس	كُوَيْت
أكُل	أنا آكُل	أتَكِيت	كِتاب	كِتابي		كِتابُك
راديكالي	أكْوادور	كيتو	مَكْسيك	كَلب	بَنْك	كَباب
سَمَك	هَمْبَرْكِر	كَج أب	مَكْدوس	لَكِن	بَكى	دينَك
كُرْكُم	لَكَ	أمَكَ	لُكُ	يَلُكُ	كِ	ألِيكِ	كاتِب	مَكْتوب

> Arabic uses ك and sometimes q as in Iraq to spell the sound of k. However, English spells the "k" sound in five ways, as in (**k**eep), (**q**uit), x=kc (an**x**ious), hard c (**c**at), or hard ch (**ch**emistry).

❹ Pick the correct shape of the letter كاف to fill in these blanks:

←

_ـا   _و _و   _و _و   _يـ _ـ _ـي   _يـ _ي   _يـو   _اقـ _ـا

_ذا   _ها   _هيـ   _بيَـ   زيَـ   _ي هـا   _ي زَ _ي   _وك

_ـرْكو   _ كيـ   _يْـكَة   كيكا   كيكو   كو _و

يـ _   بوكيـ _   _ـا _يك   بـا _يت   كا _ـاك   _اكوك

لا _وك   كالا   مَكو _   تِكْتا _   لَـ _م   لَـ _   دَ _

زَجَـ _   جو _ـر   _ تَـ _ لِفَة   فِـ _رَة   فى   يَتَـ _هَن   _ل

هَجا _   _هذا   _ذاك   _ريم   كَـ _ريم   _نسَ   رَ _ب

جابَـ _   راد   دَرسِـ _   طَلَبَـ _   أو _ـلاهوما   ألاسْـ _ـا

لاس فيـ _ـس   دَنيمارْ _   نيكارا _ وِة   أمْريـ _ـة   أمْريـ _ي

أمْريـ _يَة   _امِرَة   _ارْتون   كْلاسيـ _ـي   ذَ _ي   آلِـ _ـس

يـلوْواط   دِ _تور   دِ _تورَة   دِ _توراه   سِـ _ون   _سْرة

بْلاسْتي _   يمْياء   _وب   ألْـ _وب   _وبةُ   _وبها

سُـ _ـرْ _وَّيس   _وَيْت   أ _ل   _ل   أنا آ _ل   أتَـ _يت

_تاب   _تابي   _تابك   رادِيـ _ـالي   أ _ وادور   _يتو

مَكْسيـ _   _لب   بَـنْـ _   _باب   سَمَـ _   هَمْبَرْ _ـر   _ج أبْ

مَـ _دوس   لَـ _ن   بَـ _ى   دينَـ _   كُرْ _م   أمْ _   كَـ _ أمَك

يَدَ _

إلَيـ _

Chapter 4 — ض :D — Daad: ضاد

This Arabic letter name is Daad ضاد and it has a special deep sound of a "d". The closest English letter that can represent the sound of Daad ضاد would be a capital "d" as in (Riyadh: riyaaD رياض). The letter ضاد is a consonant and it is given the symbol of the capital "D" in this book to tell it apart from the ordinary "d" as in "do". The ضاد has four shapes: beginning ضــ, middle ـضـ, end ـض, and isolated ض:

ضــ   ـضـ   ـض   ض
ضاد   بَيضَة   بيض   رياض

❶ Read aloud slowly these Arabic words focusing on the four shapes of ضاد:

Riyaadh:	رياض	De*m*′·meh:	ضمة
eggs: be*y*D	بيض	egg: bey′·Deh	بيضة
sick: me·reeD′	مرض	sick ♀:	مريض
guest: Deyf	ضيف	guests: Di·yoof′	ضيوف
the past: maa′·Dee	ماضي	guarantee (v.):	ضَمان
run (v.): 'ir·kuD′	إركُض	hit (v.): 'iD·rub′	أضرب
white:	أبيض	security:	ضمان
tax ♀: De·ree′·beh	ضَريبة	conscious:	ضَمير
flood:	فيضان	sickness: me′·reD	مَرض
workout:	رِياضَة	necessary:	ضِروري
favor: feDl	فَضل	please:	مِن فَضْلَك
please come in/please take: 'it·fe′·Del	إتْفَضَل		
fog:	ضَباب	you:	إنتَ
you (pl)	إنْتوا	you (pl) bring:	إِنْتو تجيبون

❷ Read aloud the Daad ضاد with other learned letters five times per page:

ضا   ضاضا   ضو   ضوضو   ضي   ضيضو   ضيضي

ضيضي   ضيض   فيض   بيض   ضاض   ماض   باض

راض   فاض   فاضي   راضي   رِياضي   ماضي   ضَمَّة

ضَباب   يضرب   أبيَض   باضَت   رَضْوان   ضِرْس   ضِنون

ضَمير   إنْهَض   كُل بيض   ضَجيج   ضِدي   هَضم   هو ضَيف

مَريض   إتْفَضَل يا رِياض   لا تَضَرِب   ضا   ضَ   ضو   ضُ

ضي   ضِ   من فَضْلِك   ضَيف   أنا وأنْتَ ضِيوف   ألرِياضَة

ضِرورية   هكَذا هي ألدُنيا   ماضي   جيب ألكَباب مِن فَضْلَك   جيب

ألكَباب مِن فَضْلِك ♀   ضَباب   وميض   ضيضاض   ضيضوض

ضوضوض   ضيضض   بوضيض   ضضاض   إنْضِمام   تُفَكر

بِلا ضَوضاء   ضنون   باضِت ألدِجاجة   أنا آكُل بيض تازَة   في

ألماضي هِيَ كانَت تاكُل   رِضا   رَضى   هو مِضْطَر ياكُل   هِيَ

مِضْطَرَة تاكُل ضِياء   رِياض وَضِياء مُضْطَرين ياكلون   لَيْلى وَلُبنى

ضيوف   إضراب   أنا أرْكُض   هُوَ يَركُض   هِيَ تَرْكُض

هم يَرْكُضون

The Arabic Alphabet for English Speakers

❸ Practice writing these four shapes of the letter Daad ضاد:

ض ض ض ض

ض ض ض ض

ضاد بَيضَة بيض رياض

ض ض ض ض ض ضاد ض ض ض فض

ض ض ض ض بيض ض ض ض ماض

ضا ضاضا ضو ضوضو ضي ضيضو ضيضي

ضيضي ضيض فيض بيض ضاض ماض باض

راض فاض فاضي راضي رياضي ماضي ضَمَّة

ضَباب يضرب أبيَض باضَت رَضْوان ضِرْس

ضِنون ضَمير إنْهَض كُل بيض ضَجيج ضِدي

هَضم هو ضَيف مَريض إتْفَضَل يا رياض لا تَضَرب

ضا ضَ ضو ضُ ضي ضِ من فَضْلَك ضَيف

124

ماضي	هكَذا هِيَ ألدُنيا	ألرِّياضَة ضرورِيَة	أنا وأَنْتَ ضِيوف
ضباب	♀ جيبِ ألكَباب مِن فَضْلِك	جيب ألكَباب مِن فَضْلَك	
ضيضض	ضوضوض	ضيضاض	وَميض
ضنون	تُفَكِّر بلا ضَوضاء	إنْضِمام	ضضاض	بوضيض
تاكُل	في ألماضي هِيَ كانَت	أنا آكُل بيض تازة	باضَت ألدِجاجة
ضياء	هِيَ مِضْطَرَة تاكُل	هو مِضْطَر ياكُل	رَضى	رضا
إضراب	لَيلى ولُبنى ضيوف	رياض وَضِياء مُضْطَرين ياكلون	
هم يَرْكُضون	هِيَ تَرْكُض	هُوَ يَرْكُض	أنا أرْكُض

❹ Pick the correct shape of the letter ضاد to fill in these blanks:

ض   ضـ   ـضـ   ـض   ض
ض   ـضـ   ـضـ   ض

ضاد   بَيضَة   بيض   رياض

__ا __ا __ا __و __و __و __ي __ي __و
__ي __ي __ي __ي فـي __بيـ __ضا __ما __با
__را فا __ي فا __ي را __ي رِيا __ي ما __ي __َمَّة
__باب يـ __رب أبيَ __ت با __وان رَ __وان __رس
__نون __مير إنَّهَ __ كُل بيـ __ __جيج __دي
هَ __م هو __يف مَريـ __ إتْفَ __َل يا رِيا __ لا تَ __رب
__ا __ ضَ __و __ي ضُ __ ض مِن فَ __لَك __يف
أنا وأنْتَ __يوف ألرِيا __ـة __رورية هكَذا هي ألدُنيا ما __ي
جيب ألكَباب مِن فَ __لَك ♀ جيبِ ألكَباب مِن فَ __لَك __باب
ومي __ ضيـ __اض __ يضوض __ ضوضو __ ضيضض __
بو __يض ضضا __ إنـ __مام تُفَكر بِلا ضَو __اء __نون
با __ت ألدِجاجة أنا آكُل بيـ __ تازَة في ألما __ي هِيَ كانَت تاكُل
رِ __ا __ رَ __ى هو مِ __طَر ياكُل هِيَ مِ __طَرة تاكُل __ياء
رِيا __ وَ __ياء مُ __طَرين ياكلون لَيلى ولُبنى __يوف إ __راب
أنا أركُ __ هُوَ يَركُ __ هِيَ تَركُ __ هم يَركُ __ ون

Chapter 5 — A: ع — Aeyn: عَيْن

This Arabic letter name is Aeyn عَيْن and it has a special deep sound that is deeper than the plain "a" sound. It comes from deep in the stomach. The closest letter that can represent the sound of عَيْن would be the capital "A" as in (macaroni: meA·ke·rōo′·nee مَعْكَروني). The عَيْن is a consonant and it is given the symbol of the capital "A" in this book to tell it apart from the ordinary "a." The عَيْن has four shapes: beginning ـعـ, middle ـعـ, end ـع, and isolated ع:

عَين   أَلعَرَبي   ذيع   ذاع

❶ Read these Arabic words aloud slowly focusing on the four shapes عَيْن:

the Arabic:	أَلعَرَبي	Arabic: Aa′·ra·bee	عَرَبي
pardon:	عَفْواً	macaroni:	مَعْكَروني
Oman:	عُمان	Saudi:	سِعودي
Aden:	عَدن	Arafat:	عَرَفات
eyes/wells:	عيون	Aayn/ an eye/ a well:	عَيْن
yes (f):	نَعَم	my eyes:	عِيوني
listen:	إسْمَع	appointment:	مَوْعِد
play:	إلْعَب	teach:	عَلِّم
on:	عَلى	toy/game:	لُعْبَة
goodbye:	مَع ألسَلامَة	with:	مَع
teacher:	مُعَلِّم	restaurant:	مَطعَم
in a hurry	بِسُرْعَة	come:	تَعال
joyful:	مُمْتِع	means:	يَعْني
mad/angry:	زَعْلان	high:	عالي
natural:	طَبيعي	tired:	تَعْبان
far:	بَعيد	conscious:	واعي
fast:	سَريع	happy:	سَعيد
deep:	عَميق	slim:	رَفيع
weak:	ضَعيف	wide:	عَريض

The Arabic Alphabet for English Speakers

of course: طَبْعاً	and then: وبعدَين
four: ٤ أرْبَعة	address: عِنْوان
nine: ٩ تِسْعَة	seven: ٧ سَبْعَة
it thawed: ماع	he sold: باع
he announced: ذاع	announce: ذيع
Jesus: يسوع	issue: موضوع
you have: عِنْدَك	I have: عِنْدي
about: عَن	generally: عموما
disgrace/dishonor: عار	shame: عَيب
woman: مَرْأة	man: رَجُل

❷ Read aloud the عَيْن with other learned letters five times per page:

ذاع   ضيع   بيع   عيعي   عي   عيعو   عوعو   عو   عا

أَعْلى   عَلى   سَعيد   عيد   ضيع   بيع   واع   جاع   باع   ماع

جوعان   جوع   بَعوض   ذيعي   ذيع   أفاعي   واعي

عِنْوان   عروس   عرس   باعَت   دَلَع   لاعوب   مَوْضوع

عِع   عيع   عُع   عوع   عاع   وَبَعدين   يسوع   عالَمي

عَيب   عريض   راعي   راع   داعي   عَزيز   عَعاع   عَعع

تَعْليم   فَعْلى   فِعْل   طَمّاع   لَعَلا   نوع   ساعَة   مَع   مَعْيوب

تَعْبان   لِعب   ضَعيف   مَعْلومات   مَعْلوم   مُتَعَلِّم   مُعَلِّم

تَوَرَّع   زَرَع   هَلَع   طَبْعاً   عجب   نَوْع   ضَع   عَيْنك

The Arabic Alphabet for English Speakers

بَعيد   أَرْبَعَة   تِسْعَة   رَفيع   عِنْدي   عموماً   سَريع   عَميق   عار   وَضاع   أَنا عَرَبي.   أَنا سِعودي.   آني مِن ألسِعوديَة.   آني مو مِن ألسِعوديَة.   ألمَوضوع مو مُهِم.   مُعَلِّم ألعَرَبي مِنْ عَدَن.   إسْمَع ألرّاديو.   عَلِّم عَرَبي.   إلْعَب رِياضَة.   وَين ألمَطْعَم؟   أُريد مَعْكَروني.   عِنْدي مَوْعِد.   عَفواً، وَين هَذا إلعِنْوان؟   تَعال نِلْعِب لُعْبَة جَديدَة وَبَعْدين نِرْجَع لِلْمَطْعَم.   طَبْعاً ألجَبَل عالي وَبَعيد.   أَنا مو زَعْلان، لَكِن تَعْبان وَلازِم أَنام.   يَعْني لازِم أَنام بْسُرْعَة.   ألجاكيت عَريض   ألبايْسِكِل سَريع   ألسيّارَة سَريعَة   عِنْدَك كِتاب؟   ألرَّجُل واعي   هُوَ عِموماً سَعيد.   ألمَرأة واعِيَة.   ألمَرأة سَعيدَة.   هِيَ عموماً تَعْمِل مَعَه.   ألمَوْضوع هُوَ عَن ألوَعي ألعَميق مو عَن ألسِعادة.

❸ Practice writing these four shapes of the letter عَيْن:

ع   ع   ـع   ـعـ   ـعـ
ع   ع   ـع   ـعـ   ـعـ
عاد   يَعي   بيع   باع

ـعـ   ـعـ   ـعـ   ـعـ   ـعـ   عاد   يَعي

ـع   ـع   ـع   ـع   ـع   بيع   باع

عيعي	عيعو	عي	عوعو	عو	عاعا	عا
جاع	ضيع	بيع	سَعيد	عيد	عود	عوز	عاد	عاف
ذاع	ضيع	بيع	عيعي	عي	عيعو	عوعو	عا
عَلى	عيد سَعيد	ضيع	بيع	واع	جاع	باع	ماع
جوع	بَعوض	ذيعي	ذيع	أفاعي	واعي	أعْلى
عرس	باعَت	دَلَع	لاعوب	مَوْضوع	جوعان
عَع	عاع	وَبَعدين	يَسوع	عالَمي	عِنْوان	عروس
داعي	عَزيز	عَعاع	عَعع	عِع	عيع	عُع	عوع
ساعَة	مَعَ	مَعْيوب	عَيب	عَريض	راعي	راع
مُتَعَلِّم	مُعَلِّم	تَعْليم	فَعَلى	فِعْل	طَمّاع	لَعَلا	نوع
عَيْنك	تَعْبان	لِعب	ضَعيف	مَعْلومات	مَعْلوم
بَعيد	تَوَرَّع	زَرَع	هَلَع	طَبْعاً	عجب	نَوْع	ضَع
عَميق	سَريع	عموماً	عِنْدي	رَفيع	تِسْعَة	أرْبَعة

عار   وَضاع   أنا عَرَبي.   أنا سِعودي.   آني من ألْسِعودِيَة.

آني مو من ألْسِعودِيَة.   ألْمَوضوع مو مُهِم.   مُعَلِّم ألْعَرَبي مِنْ

عَدَن.   إَسْمَع ألْراديو.   عَلِّم عَرَبي.   إلْعَب رياضَة.   وَين

ألْمَطْعَم؟   أريد مَعْكَروني.   عِنْدي مَوْعِد.   عَفواً، وَين هَذا؟

الْعِنْوان؟   تَعال نِلْعَب لُعْبَة جَديدَة وَبَعْدين نِرْجَع لِلْمَطْعَم.   طِبْعاً

ألْجَبَل عالي وَبَعيد.   أنا مو زَعْلان، لَكِن تَعْبان وَلازِم أنام.   يَعْني

لازِم أنام بْسُرْعَة.   ألْجاكيت عَريض   ألْبايْسِكِل سَريع

ألْسَيارَة سَريعَة   عِنْدَك كِتاب؟   ألْرَجُل واعي   هُوَ عِموماً

سَعيد.   ألْمَرأة واعِيَة وَسَعيدَة.   هِيَ عموماً تَعْمَل مَعَه في سيناء.

ألْمَوْضوع هُوَ عَن ألْوَعي ألْعَميق، مو عَن ألْسِعادة.   لِلْإسْتِماع

The Arabic Alphabet for English Speakers

❹ Pick the correct shape of the letter عَيْن to fill in these blanks:

ع عـ ـعـ ـع

ع ـعـ ـعـ ـعـ

باع   بيع   يَعي   عاد

ضيـ__ بيـ__ـي عيـ__ـي _ـي _و_ـو _و_ـو _ـا

_يد ضيـ__ بيـ__ وا__ جا__ با__ ما__ ذا

ذيـ__ـي ذيـ__ أفا__ـي وا__ـي أ__لى __لى سَـ__ـيد

دَلَـ__ لا__وب موضو__ جو__ـان جو__ بَـ__وض

يسو__ __المي __نوان __روس __رس با__ـت

__ـِ عيـ__ __ عُـ __ عو __ عَـ عا وَبَـ__دين

__ريض را__ـي را__ـي دا__ـي __ـزيز __اع عـ__ع

طَماً __لا __ نو سا__ة مَـ__ __يوب مَـ__يب

مَـ__لوم مُتَـ__لِّم مُـ__لِّم تَـ__ليم فَـ__لى فِـ__ل

__ضَـ __يْنك تَـ__بان لِـ__ب ضَـ__يف مَـ__لومات

بَـ__يد تَوَرَّ__ زَرَ__ هَلَ__ طَبـ__اً __جب نَو__

__ميق __سريـ__ __موماً __ندي رَفيـ__ تِسْـ__ة أرْبَـ__ة

آني من آلسِـ__ودِيَة. أنا سِـ__ودي. أنا __رَبي. وضا__ وا__ار

مُـ__لِّم ألـ__رَبي من آني مو من آلسِـ__ودِية. ألمَوضو__ مو مُهم.

وَين. إلّاـ__ب رياضَة. __لِّم __رَبي. إسْمَـ__ ألرّاديو. __دَن.

132

أَلْمَطْ_م؟   أُريد مَ_كَروني.   _نْدي مَوْ_د.   _فواً، وَين هَذا إلـ_نْوان؟   تَ_ـال نِلْـ_ب لُـ_بَة جَديدَة وَبَـ_دين نِرْجَـ_ لِلْمَطْ_م.

طِبْ_ـاً أَلْجَبَل _ـالي وَبَـ_يد.   أَنا مو زَ_لان، لَكِن تَ_بان وَلازِم أَنام. يَـ_ني لازِم أَنام بْسُرْ_ـة.   أَلْجاكَيت _رِيض   أَلْبايْسِكِل سَريـ_

أَلسَيارَة سَريـ_ـة   _نْدَك كِتاب؟   أَلْرَجُل وا_ـي   هُوَ _موماً سَـ_يد.   أَلْمَرأة وا_ية.   أَلْمَرأة سَـ_يدَة.   هِيَ _موماً تَـ_ـمِل مَـ_ـه.   أَلْمَوْضوع _ _ ـن أَلْوَ_ـي أَلْـ_ميق مو عَن أَلْسِـ_ـادة.   شُكْراً لِلإسْتِما_.

Chapter 6 — ش sh: شين sheen'

This Arabic letter name is sheen شين and it sounds like the English "sh" as in "she." The شين is a consonant and it is given the symbol "sh" in this book as in (shampoo: shaam'·boo شامْبو). The letter شين has four shapes: beginning شـ, middle ـشـ, end ـش, and isolated ش:

ش	ـش	ـشـ	شـ
دوش	عيش	مَشِكَن	شين

❶ Read these Arabic words slowly focusing on the four shapes of sheen شين:

shower:	دوش	live (v.):	عيش
I live:	أَعيش	fascist:	فاشي
pick up:	شيل	pick up ♀:	شيلي
comprehensive:	شامِل	walk/get moving:	إمْشي
tea:	شاي	thing:	شي
anything:	أي شي	everything:	كُل شي
degree/affidavit:	شَهادِة	popular:	مَشْهور
hair:	شَعر	poetry:	شِعر
skin:	بَشَرَة	humans:	بَشَر
month:	شَهر	honeymoon:	شَهْر إلْعَسَل
February:	شْباط	October:	تِشرين ألأَوَل
apricots:	مِشمِش	candy:	شوكولاتَة
shaddah:	شِدَة	thanks:	شُكْراً
air condition:	أيْرِكِنْدِشِن	Gyro:	شاوِرْما
street:	شارِع	10: ١٠	عَشْرَة
Decimal:	عِشري	14: ١٤	أرْبَعَة
17: ١٧	سَبْعَة عَشر	chess:	شِطْرِنْج
a little bit:	شْوِيَه	a little bit of:	شْوَيَة
why (g):	ليش؟	not (e):	مِش
how much (g):	بيش	what (g):	أيش

this isn't (e):	مَهوش	there isn't (e):	مَفيش
there is no tea (e):	مَفيش شاي	what? (g):	شِنو؟
what is it (g):	شَكو؟	forget it/free:	بَلاش
now (g):	هَسَة	must:	لازِم
what should (g):	شلازِم	I do/ I make:	أَسَوّي
come:	تَعال	how're you (g):	شْلونَك
feelings:	شَعور	your feelings:	شِعورَك
the same thing:	نَفْس إلْشي	nightgown (g):	دِشْداشَة
cheerful/smiley:	بَشوش	how (e):	إزي؟
how're you:	إزَيَك	how're you:	كَيْفَك؟
long lived/lived:	عاش	the people:	ألْشَعَب
communist:	شِيوعي	communism:	شِيوعِيَة
capitalist:	رَإسْمالي	capitalism:	رَإسْمالية
sun:	شَمْس	sunrise:	شِروق ألْشَمْس
shower:	دوش	smart:	شاطِر
Venus:	فينوس	drink (v.):	إشْرَب
he drinks:	يَشْرَب	we drink:	نَشْرَب
buy:	إشْتِري	he buys:	يَشْتَري
see:	شوف	he sees:	يَشوف
honorable:	شَريف	honorable ♀:	شَريْفَة
problem ♀:	مُشكِلَة	problems:	مَشاكِل
society:	مُجْتَمَع	social:	إجْتِماعي
political:	سِياسي	scientific:	عِلْمي

The Arabic Alphabet for English Speakers

The Arabic Alphabet for English Speakers

❷ Read aloud the شين with other learned letters, five times per page:

←

شا   شاش   شو   شوشو   شي   شيشي   شيش   شيشَة

دشاشي   فاشي   ماشي   كاش   عاش   فيش   مَفيش   دوش

شوش   شُش   شاش شَش   شيش   شِش   شيكاكو   ناشْفِل

ناشْفيل   واشِنْطِن   مَشِكَن   شَنْدَلير   مِتْسوبيشي   حَشيش

شيل   شامْبو   شامِل   شاي   شي   شَهادَة   إمْشي   شَهْر

شَعَر   شِعِر   بَشر   بَشَرَة   عاش ألْشَعب   شهر شباط   شهر

العسل   تشرين   لَيْش؟   لَيْش شَكو؟   أَيْش؟   أَيْش ألْمَوضوع؟

إِشْ   بَيْش؟   بَيْش ألْسَنْدَويج؟   شْلازِم نِشْرَب؟   دا مَهوش شيش

كَباب.   مِش مِشْمِش   شلون   شْلونَك؟   شْلونِج؟   شِنو؟

شْلون شِعورَك يا رَشيد؟   شِعورَك وَشِعوري نَفْس إلْشي.   إِنْتَ مش

بَشوش أَليوم.   مِش مُشْكِلَة.   تعال نِمْشي وناكُل شاوِرْمَة أَو طَعْمِيَة.

❸ Practice writing these four shapes of the letter شين:

ش   ش   شـ   ـشـ

شاي   بُشرى   ماشي   عاش

ش ـشـ شـ ش   شاي   ش ـشـ شـ ش   بُشرى

_____

ش ش ش ش   ماشي   ش ش ش ش   عاش

_____

شيشَة	شيش	شيشي	شي	شوشو	شو	شاش	شا
مَفيش	فيش	عاش	كاش	ماشي	فاشي	دشاشي	
شيكاكو	شِش	شيش	شاش شَش	شُش	شوش	دوش	
شَنْدَليِر	شيلي	مَشِكَن	واشِنْطِن	ناشْفيل	ناشْفِل		
شي	شاي	شامِل	شامْبو	شيل	حَشيش	مِتْسوبيشي	
بَشَرَة	بَشِر	شِعِر	شَعَر	شَهْر	إمْشي	شَهادَة	
لَيْش؟	تشرين	شهر العسل	شهر شباط	عاش الْشَعب			
بَيْش	بَيْش؟	إش	أَيْش ألْمَوضوع؟	أَيْش؟	لَيْش شَكو؟		
مِش	دا مَهوش شيش كَباب.	شْلازِم نِشْرَب؟	ألْسَنْدَويِج؟				
شْلون	شِنو؟	شْلونِج؟	شْلونَك؟	شلون	مِشْمِش		
مِش مُشْكِلَة.	شِعورَك وَشِعوري نَفْس إلْشي.	شِعورَك يا رَشيد؟					

Chapter 7 — H: ح — Haa': حاء

This Arabic letter name is Haa' حاء and it has a special deeper sound than the ordinary "h". The حاء is often represented by an "h" in English as in (alcohol: ki·Hool' كحول). The letter حاء is a consonant and it is given the symbol of the capital "H" in this book to tell it apart from the ordinary "h" as in haa' هاء. The حاء has four shapes: beginning ح‍, middle ‍ح‍, end ‍ح, and isolated ح:

حـ   ‍حـ   ‍ح   ح
حُب   لَحم   مِلح   روح

❶ Read these Arabic words aloud slowly focusing on the four shapes حاء:

alcohol:	كِحول	grass:	حَشيش
hello:	مَرْحَبا	bathroom/bath:	حَمّام
museum:	مَتْحَف	theater:	مَسْرَح
wall:	حائِط	one/someone: ١	واحِد
11: ١١	إحْدى عَشَر	21: ٢١	واحِد وعِشرون
allow me please:	إسْمَح لي	fet'·Heh:	فَتْحَة
sweet:	حِلو	sad:	حَزين
happy:	فَرْحان	ambitious:	طَموح
red:	أَحْمَر	respectable:	مُحْتَرَم
forgiving:	مُسامِح	neutral:	مُحايِد
placed:	مَحْطوط	lovely:	مَحْبوب
love:	حُب	my lover:	حَبيبي
sea:	بَحْر	two seas:	بَحْرين
ocean:	مُحيط	freedom:	حُرِيَة
dream (n.):	حِلْم	iron:	حَديد
shoe:	حِذاء	animal:	حَيوان
war:	حَرْب	wars:	حُروب
government:	حِكومَة	political party:	حِزْب
the bill/math:	إلْحِساب	salt:	مِلْح

meat:	لَحْم	milk:	حَليب
laugh (v):	إِضْحَك	go:	روح
insist:	لِح	put	حُط
until/so/for:	حَتّى	most likely:	حَتْماً
my life:	حَياتي	life ♀:	حَياة
now (Gulf Dialect):	إِلْحين	in the morning:	

❷ Read the Haa' حاء with other learned letters aloud five times per page:

ح ـح ـحـ حـ

حاء   لَحم   مِلح   روح

حا   حو   حي   حوحو   حاحي   حيحي   حاحي   حيح   حَح

حُح   حِح   حيح   حُر   حَبيبي   واحِد   فَرْحان   إِضْحَك

حُرِيَة   حِلم   حِكومة   أَحْمَر   مَرْحَبا   حِروب   أُحِب   عَبد

أَلْحَليم   هُوَ مَحْبوب اَلْجَماهير   راحَت   طَحين   شَحيح   كحول

نَحيف   بَحر   بَحرين   مَتْحَف   مَسْرَح   مُحيط   حَمّام

حِزْب   حائِط   حَزين   إِحدا عَشَر   حَتْماً   حَتّى   حَليب

لاح   راح   روح   طاح   سائِح   أَتاح   ضاحِيَة   إِلْحِساب

مِن فَضْلَك   إِسْمَح لي   إِكْتِب حاء

The Arabic Alphabet for English Speakers

❸ Practice writing these four shapes of the letter Haa' حاء:

ح　ح　ح　ح　ح
ح　ح　ح　ح

حاء　لحم　ملح　روح

حا　حو　حي　حوحو　حيحي　حاحي　حيحي　حيح

حَح　حُح　حِح　حيح　حُر　حَبيبي　واحِد　فَرْحان

إضحَك　حُرِّية　حِلم　حِكومَة　حِروب　أحْمَر　مَرْحَبا

أحِب عَبد ألْحَليم　هُوَ مَحْبوب ألْجَماهير　راحَت　طَحين

شَحيح　كِحول　نَحيف　بَحر　بَحْرين　مَتْحَف　مَسْرَح

مُحيط　حَمّام　حِزْب　حائِط　حَزين　أحدا عَشَر

حَتْماً　حَتى　حَليب　لاح　راح　روح　طاح　سائِح

أتاح　ضاحِيَة　ألْحِساب مِن فَضْلَك　إسْمح لي　إكْتِب حاء

140

❹ Pick the correct shape of the letter حاء to fill in these blanks:

د ـد ـحـ ح
ح ـحـ ـح ح
ح ـح ـحـ ح

حاء   لحم   ملح   روح

ـــا   ـــو   ـــي   ـــيـــ   ـــو   ـــو   ـــي   ـــا   ـــي

ـــر   ـــيـــ   ـــيـــ   ـــَ   ـــُ   ـــِ   ـــي   ـــي

ـــبيبي   وا ـــد   فَرْـــان   إضـــك   ـــرِية   ـــلم

ـــكومة   ـــروب   أـــمَر   مَرْـــبا   أـــب عَبد ألـ ـــليم

هُوَ مَـــبوب ألْجَماهير   راـــت   طَـــين   شَـــيـــ

كِـــول   نَـــيف   بَـــر   بَـــرين   مَثـــف   مَسْرَـــ

مُـــيط   ـــمَّام   ـــزْب   ـــائط   ـــزين   أـــدا

عَشَر   ثُمَاً   ـــتى   ـــليب   لا   را   رو   رو

طا   سائـــ   أتا   ضاـــية   إلـ ـــساب مِن فضْلَك

إسْمـــ لي   إكْتِب ـــاء   إلـ ـــين

➤ Some parts of speech:

noun:	إسْم	verb:	فِعْل
subject/doer:	فاعِل	object:	مَفْعول بِهِ
human:	إنْسان	animal:	حَيوان
nonliving:	جَماد		

141

❹ **Pick the correct shape of the letter شين to fill in these blanks:**

ش ‌شـ ‌ـشـ ‌ـش
ش ‌شـ ‌ـشـ ‌ـش
عاش   هش   نشر   شاي

__ـا شا __ـو __ـو __ـو __ـي __ـي __ـي
__ـيـ __ة __اي __ي فا__ي ما__ي كا__ي __ـا عا__
فا__ي مَفيـ__ دو__ __ـيـ __و __ا
و__ __ شيـ__ يكاكو نا__ فيل وا__ نْطِن مَ__كَن
__يلي __نْدَلير مِتْسوبي__ـي حَ__ـيـ__ __يل
__ـامْبو __امِل __اي __ي __هادَة إمـ__ـي
__هْر __عَر __عِر __ـر بَ__رَة عا إلـ__عب
__هر باط __هر العسل ت__رين لَيـ__؟ لَيـ__
__كو؟ أَيْ__؟ أَيْ__ أَلْمَوضوع؟ إ__ بَيْ__؟ بَيْ__
أَلسَنْدْويج؟ __لازِم نِ__رَب؟ دا مَهو __يـ__ كَباب.
مِ__مِ__مِ__نو __لون لونَك؟ __لونج؟ __نو؟
__لون __عورَك يا رَ__يد؟ __عورَك و__عوري نَفْس إلـ__ـي.
إنْتَ مَ__بَ__و__ أَليوم. مِ__ مُ__كِلَة. تعال نِمْ__ـي وناكُل __اورْمَة أو طَعْمِيَة.

Chapter 8 — Numbers: أَرْقام (101 – 1000000)

Read these Arabic numbers from right to left ←

Just like English, saying 101 in Arabic is "one hundred and one." Thus, saying 101 is (miyyeh wiwaaHid مِيَّة وواحِد). Usually, Arabic speakers say مَيَّة but they write مائة, which still means one hundred.

English	number
101:	١٠١
102:	١٠٢
110:	١١٠
111:	١١١
120:	١٢٠
121:	١٢١
130:	١٣٠
140:	١٤٠
150:	١٥٠
160:	١٦٠
170:	١٧٠
180:	١٨٠
190:	١٩٠
200:	٢٠٠
201:	٢٠١
298:	٢٩٨
300:	٣٠٠
400:	٤٠٠
500:	٥٠٠
600:	٦٠٠
700:	٧٠٠
800:	٨٠٠
900:	٩٠٠
1000:	١٠٠٠
1001	١٠٠١
1100	١١٠٠
2000:	٢٠٠٠
3000:	٣٠٠٠
4000:	٤٠٠٠
5000:	٥٠٠٠
6000:	٦٠٠٠
10,000:	١٠٠٠٠
100,000:	١٠٠٠٠٠
million:	١٠٠٠٠٠٠

Read these Arabic numbers from right to left ←

Just like English, saying 201 in Arabic is "two hundred and one." Thus, saying 201 is (maa´··e·taan wiwaaHid مائتَان وواحد). Usually, Arabic speakers say مَيَّة but they write مائة, which still means one hundred.

English	number
201:	٢٠١
202:	٢٠٢
210:	٢١٠
211:	٢١١
220:	٢٢٠
221:	٢٢١
230:	٢٣٠
240:	٢٤٠
250:	٢٥٠
260:	٢٦٠
270:	٢٧٠
280:	٢٨٠
290:	٢٩٠
300:	٣٠٠
301:	٣٠١
398:	٣٩٨
400:	٤٠٠
500:	٥٠٠
600:	٦٠٠
900:	٨٠٠
2000:	٢٠٠٠
3000:	٣٠٠٠
3001	٣٠٠١
4000:	٤٠٠٠
4000	٤١٠٠

PART FIVE
The Last Six Letters

Name	Symbol as in	Isolated	End	Middle	Beginning
thaa': ثاء	th: ether: eether: إيثَر	ث	ث	ـثـ	ثـ
khaa': خاء	kh: Bach: baakh: باخ	خ	ـخ	ـخـ	خـ
Saad: صاد	S: bus: baaS باص	ص	ـص	ـصـ	صـ
Zaa': ظاء	Z: Dubai: Zubey ظُبَي	ظ	ظ	ظ	ظ
gheyn: غين	gh: Brach: braagh بْراغ	غ	ـغ	ـغـ	غـ
qaaf: قاف	q: Iraq: Airaaq عِراق	ق	ـق	ـقـ	قـ

Isolated	End	Middle	Beginning
ث	ث	ـثـ	ثـ
خ	ـخ	ـخـ	خـ
ص	ـص	ـصـ	صـ
ظ	ظ	ظ	ظ
غ	ـغ	ـغـ	غـ
ق	ـق	ـقـ	ق

Chapter 1 — th: ث — thaa': ثاء

This Arabic letter name is thaa' ثاء and it sounds just like the English "th" as in "bath". The ث is a consonant and it is given the symbol "th" in this book as in (Judith: joo·deth جودَث). The ث has four shapes: beginning ثـ, middle ـثـ, end ـث, and isolated ث:

ث   ـث   ـثـ   ثـ

ثاء   كَثير   حَديث   تُراث

❶ Read these Arabic words aloud slowly focusing on the four shapes of ثاء:

thaa':	ثاء	then:	ثُمَ
ice/snow:	ثَلْج	garlic:	ثوم
a lot/very:	كَثير	more:	أَكْثَر
ether:	إيثَر	triangle:	مُثَلَث
trilogy:	ثُلاثِية	third:	ثالِث
third of all:	ثالِثاً	for example:	مَثَلاً
second:	ثاني	second of all:	ثانِياً
furniture:	أثاث	culture:	تُراث
revolution:	ثَوْرة	revolutionary:	ثَوْري
revolutionist:	ثائِر	stable:	ثابِت
he inherits:	يَرِث	modern:	حَديث
letter:	حَرْف	letters:	حِروف
vowel:	حَرْف عِلّة	Herekaat:	حَرَكات

The Arabic Alphabet for English Speakers

❷ Read the ثاء with other learned letters aloud five times per page:

ثا ثا ثاثا ثو ثو ثوثو ثيثو ثي ثيثي ثيث هيث
ثاث أثاث ثالِث ثالِث ثلاثِة ثالوث ثالِثا ثاء كَثير
أكْثَر حَديث تُراث ثيثاث ثوثاث ثيثث بوثوث بوثيث
بوثاث باثيث ثاثيث ثاثاث ثاثوث لاثوث ثالاث
ثَمَر ثُمَ ثوم ثَلْج مُثَلَج إيثَر مثلاً ثانِياً ثاني
مُثَلَّث أثاث تُراث ثَوْرَة ثَوري ثائِر ثابِت لَيْث
عاث عِث عَبَث رَث كَراث يَحِث يَبْحَث باحِث
باحِثة إسْتِغاث مُلَثَّم ثابِت مُثَبَّت ثَمانية رَثاء يَرِث
وِراثَة حَيث ثَمين

147

The Arabic Alphabet for English Speakers

❸ Practice writing the four shapes of ثاء:

ثـ   ثـ   ثـ   ثـ

ثـ ثـ ثـ ثـ ثاء   ثـ ثـ ثـ ثـ حّديث

بث ث ث ث ث   ث ث ث ث عاث

ثا ثا ثاثا ثو ثوثو ثي ثي ثيثي ثيث

هيث ثاث أثاث ثالث ثالثَة ثلاثة ثالوث ثالِثا

ثاء   كثير   أكْثَر   حَديث   تُراث   ثيثاث   ثوثوث   ثيثث

بوثوث   بوثيث   باثيث   ثاثيث   ثاثاث   ثاثوث

ثاثاث   لاثوث   ثالات   ثَمَر   ثُمَّ   ثوم   ثَلْج   مُثَلَّج

إيْثَر   مثلاً   ثانياً   ثاني   مُثَلَّث   أثاث   تُراث

ثَوْرَة   ثَوْري   ثائِر   ثابت   لَيْث   عاث   عِث   عَبَث

رَث   كَراث   يَحِث   يَبْحَث   باحِث   باحِثَة   إسْتَغاث

مُلَثَّم   ثابت   مُثْبَت   ثَمانية   رَثاء   يَرث   وراثَة   حَيث

❹ Pick the correct shape of the letter ثاء to fill in these blanks:

ث ث ث ث

ث ث ث ث

ثاء   كَثير   حَديث   تُراث

←

__ا __ا __ا __و __و __و __يـ__و __ي

__يـ__ي __ي __ا __أ __ا هِي

__الِ __الِ __ا __اء __الِ __الِا __الو __لا __ة __الِ __ر   أكـ__ر   كـ__ير   __اء   __الِ__ا   __الو   __لا __ة   __الِ

__ي __و __و __يـ__ا __راً   حَدي__

__ا __يـ __ا __يـ بو __ا   بو__يـ

__الا __ا __و   __لا   __ا __ا   __ا __و   __ا __ا

__مَ__لاً   إيـ__ر   مُـ__لَج   __لْج __وم __مَ__ر

__وْرَة   __راً   __ا __ا   أ   مُـ__لَـ   __اني   __انِياً

__بَ __عِ __ا __يْ__ابت   __ائِر   __وْري

__ة باجِـ__ة   باجِـ__   يَبْحَ__   يَحِ__   كَراً   __رَ

رَ__اء   __مانْيِة   مُـ__بَت   __ابِت   مُلَـ__م   إسْتَغا__

__بو   __مين   حَيْ__ة   وِرا__ة   يَرِ__

149

Chapter 2 — kh: خ — khaa': خاء

This Arabic letter name is khaa' خاء and it has a special nasal sound. The خ is often represented in "kh" in English as in (khaki: khaa·kee خاكي). Typically, English speakers pronounce the "kh" like "k" wherein the "h" is silent. The letter خاء is a consonant and it is given the symbol "kh" in this book. The خ has four shapes: beginning خـ, middle ـخـ, end ـخ, and isolated خ:

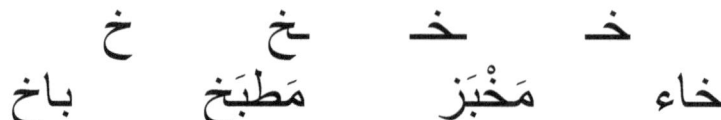

❶ Read these Arabic words aloud slowly focusing on the four shapes of خاء:

khaa':	خاء	ach:	باخ
kitchen:	مَطْبَخ	I cook:	أطْبُخ
bread:	خُبْز	bakery:	مَخْبَز
store/storage:	مَخْزَن	mustard:	خَردَل
melons:	بَطيخ	a melon:	بَطيخَة
plums: khōokh:	خوخ	a plum:	خوخَة
lettuce:	خَس	cucumbers:	خيار
vinegar:	خَل	five:	خَمسَة
a sheep:	خَروف	pig:	خَنزير
news:	أخبار	singular of news:	خَبَر
thick:	ثَخين	ridiculous:	سَخيف
Khartoum:	خَرطوم	empty/ vacant:	خالي
light weight:	خَفيف	lighter:	أخَف
green:	أخضَر	khaki:	خاكي
mixed:	مَخبوط	scary:	مُخيف
afraid:	خايف	be afraid:	خاف
I get afraid:	أخاف	untidy:	مخربَط
dangerous:	خَطِر	danger:	خَطَر

let me:	خَليني	trap:	فَخ
brother:	أَخ	public speech:	خِطاب
matches:	شِخاط	take:	خُذ
tip for waiter:	بَخْشيش	autumn:	خَريف
sound of water:	خَرير	sound of rain:	زُخاخ أَلمَطر
always alive:	خالِد	The Gulf:	أَلخَليج
out/outside:	خارِج	in/inside:	داخِل
history:	تاريخ	masochist:	مازوخي
not active:	خامِل	octopus:	أَخطَبوط
wood:	خَشب	coarse:	خَشن
toilet/wilderness:	خَلاء	he entered:	دَخَل
malignant:	خَبيث	for my sake:	لخاطري
uncle (mother's brother):	خال	my uncle:	خالي
my mother's sister:	خالتي	this is (e):	دَه

❷ Read the خ with other learned letters aloud five times per page:

خَا خَا خَاخَا خَو خَو خَوخَو خِيخَو خِي خِيخِي

خِيخ خَاء خَوخ دَاخ بَاخ شِيخ أَخ أَخِي آخ خَال

خُذ خِلاصَة دَوخ مُخ فَخ رَخ خَرْطوم خَلِيج

خَاكِي خِطَاب خِطَابَات مَخْبوط مْخَرْبَط مُخِيف خَايِف

أَخَاف خَطَر خَفِيف أَخَف خَرِيف خَمْخَم زُخَاخ خَيل

خَلِيل إِخْتَفَى شِخَاط مَطْبَخ إِطْبُخ خَرْدَل خُبْز مَخْبَز

مُخْتَبَر خَس خِيَار خَل خِضْرَاوَات بَطِيخ بَطِيخَة

بَخْشِيش خَالتِي أَخْضَر مَخْتَلَط فَاخِر خَائِر خَابِت

مَخْلَمَة مَخْطوف رَخَاء مَخْمَل خ خَخ خُخ خِخ

❸ Practice writing these four shapes of the letter خاء:

خـ ـخـ ـخـ خ
خ ـخ ـخ خـ

خاء   مَخْبَز   مَطْبَخ   باخ

خا   خا   خاخا   خو   خو   خوخو   خيخو   خي   خيخي

خيخ   خاء   خوخ   داخ   باخ   شيخ   أخ   أخي   آخ

خال   خُذ   خِلاصة   دوخ   مُخ   فَخ   رَخ   خَرْطوم

خَليج   خاكي   خِطاب   خِطابات   مَخْبوط   مُخَرْبَط

مُخيف   خايف   أخاف   خَطَر   خَفيف   أخَف   خَريف

خَمْخَم   زُخاخ   خَيل   خَليل   إخْتَفى   شِخاط   مَطْبَخ

إطبُخ   خَرْدَل   خَبْز   مُخْتَبَر   خَس   خيار   خَل

خِضْراوات   بَطيخ   بَطيخة   خالتي   أخْضَر   خخخ

فاخر   خائر   خابت   مَخْلَمة   مَخْطوف   رَخاء   مَخْمَل

After reading and understanding the above words, try reading the same words again but without the short vowels or other symbols. This type of reading is to prepare you to read other written text in Arabic:

khaa':	خاء	Bach:	باخ
kitchen:	مطبخ	I cook:	أطبخ
bread:	خبز	bakery:	مخبز
store/storage:	مخزن	mustard:	خردل
melons:	بطيخ	a melon:	بطيخة
plums: khōokh:	خوخ	a plum:	خوخة
lettuce:	خس	cucumbers:	خيار
vinegar:	خل	five:	خمسة
a sheep:	خروف	pig:	خنزير
news:	أخبار	singular of news:	خبر
thick:	ثخين	ridiculous:	سخيف
Khartoum:	خرطوم	hollow/empty:	خالي
light weight:	خفيف	lighter:	أخَف
green:	أخضر	khaki:	خاكي
mixed:	مخبوط	scary:	مخيف
afraid:	خايف	be afraid:	خاف
I get afraid:	أخاف	untidy:	مخربط
dangerous:	خطر	danger:	خطر
let me:	خليني	trap:	فخ
brother:	أخ	public speech:	خطاب
matches:	شخاط	take:	خذ
tip for waiter:	بخشيش	autumn:	خريف
sound of water:	خرير	sound of rain:	زخاخ ألمطر

154

always alive:	خالد	The Gulf:	ألخليج
out/outside:	خارج	inside:	داخل
history:	تاريخ	masochist:	مازوخي
not active:	خامل	octopus:	أخطبوط
wood:	خشب	coarse:	خشن
toilet/wilderness:	خلاء	he entered:	دخل
malignant:	خبيث	for my sake:	لخاطري
uncle (mother's brother):	خال	my uncle:	خالي
my mother's sister:	خالتي	this is (e):	ده

❹ Pick the correct shape of the letter خاء to fill in these blanks:

خـ ـخـ ـخ خ
خ ـخ ـخـ خـ

ـا ـا ـي ـا ـو ـو ـو ـي ـو ـا

ـي ـي ـيـ ـو ـاء ـ دا ـ بـا ـ شيـ

أ ـ أ ـي ـ آ ـ ال ـ ذ ـ لاصة دو ـ مُـ

ـ فـَ ـ رَ ـ رْطوم ـ ليج ـ اكي ـ طاب ـ طابات

مَـ ـ بوط مُـ ـ رْبَط مُـ ـ يف ـ ايف أ ـ اف ـ طَر

ـ فيف أ ـ ف ـ ريف ـ مـ ـ م زُ ـ ا ـ يل ـ ليل

إ ـ تَفى شِـ ـ اط مَطبَـ ـ إطبُـ ـ رْدَل ـ بْز مُـ ـ تَبَر

ـ س ـ يار ـ ل ـ ضراوات بطيـ ـ بطيـ ـ ة

ـ التي أ ـ ضَر فا ـ ر ـ ائر ـ ابت مَـ ـ لَمَة مَـ ـ طوف

رَ ـ اء مَـ ـ مَل بَـ ـ شيش مُـ ـ تَلَط نُـ ـ بَة مُـ ـ تَلَط

فَـ ـ ور

| Chapter 3 | ص :S | صاد :Saad |

This Arabic letter name is Saad صاد and it has a special sound. The closest English letter that can represent the sound of Saad صاد is the "s" as in "sum". In English, the sound of "s" in the words "see" and "sum" are different. The of Saad صاد sounds more like the in "sum" and less like the "s" in "see". The sound of Saad صاد is often represented by an "s" in English, as in (humus: Hu·muS: خُمُص). The letter Saad صاد is a consonant and its symbol in this book is a capital "S" to tell it apart from the ordinary "s." The Saad صاد has four shapes: beginning ـصـ, middle ـصـ, end ـص, and isolated ص:

صــ ـصــ ـص ص

صاد مِصْر شَخْص باص

❶ Read these Arabic words aloud slowly focusing on the four shapes صاد:

thief:	لِص	thieves:	لِصوص
summer:	صَيف	clinic:	مُستَوصِف
difficult:	صَعب	exclusive:	خاص
private:	خِصوصي	especially:	خاصَة
bus:	باص	Egypt:	مِصر
became:	صار	become:	صير
incorrigible/stuck:	مُستَعْصي	accidents:	إصطِدام
person:	شَخص	personality:	شَخصِيَة
see (e):	بُص	little light:	بَصيص
baldheaded:	أصْلَع	finger:	إصبَع
soap:	صابون	cockroach:	صَرصور
glass:	كلاص	onions:	بَصَل
quail:	عَصْفور	hush:	هِص
prayer:	صَلاة	pray (v.):	صَلّي
he prayed:	صَلّى	he fasted:	صام
cross:	صَليب	patient:	صَبور
Friday:	جُمعَة	Sunday:	أحَد
final fate:	مَصير	eco:	صَدى

statue of pagans:	صَنَم	correct/true:	صَحيح
picture:	صورَة	sound:	صوط
half:	نُص	concept:	مُصطَلَح
word root (infinitive form):	مَصدَر	adjective:	صِفة
letter:	حَرف	letters:	حِروف
consonant:	حَرف صَحيح	vowel:	حَرف عِلَة
vowels:	حِروف أَلْعِلَة	Arabic symbols:	حَرَكات
word:	كَلِمَة	sentence:	جُملَة
these (e):	دول	this (e):	دَه

❷ Read aloud the ص with other learned letters five times per each page:

←

صَا صو صِي صَاصَا صوصو صَاصو صِيصو صِي
صِيصِي صوص صَاص لَاص بَاص صَلْصَة خَاص
خِصوصِي خَاصَةً صَاد مُصطفى صَدى بُص صَار
مِصر شَخص شَخْصِية لِصوص بَصِيص صَلَاح نَاصِر
صَباح إصْطِدام صَيف مَصِيف حُمْصِي صَابون
وارصو كْلَاص مَصِير مَصدَر مُصطَلَح أَصْبِع بَصَل
صَحِيح إنْصاف صَاص صَص صوص صُص صِيص
صِص دَه بَصَل بُص دَه عِصْفور صَرصور بَصِيص صِير
هُص وِبُص دَه لُص شَخص صَعب صَار مِش شَخصِيَة صَعْبَة
دَه مِسْتَوصِف خِصوصِي مِش عِمومِي إمور مِستَعصِيَة أصْلَع
صَبور دَه حَرف صَحِيح دَه حَرف عِلَة دُل حَرَكات صَاد
مَصنَع في مَصر دَه نُص ونُص مَصِير شَعب صومال إصْبَع
صَا صَ صو صُ صِي صِ

✺Read these same above words without the Herekaat حَرَكات:

thief:	لص	thieves:	لصوص
summer:	صيف	clinic:	مستوصف
difficult:	صعب	exclusive:	خاص
private:	خصوصي	especially:	خاصة
bus:	باص	Egypt:	مصر
incorrigible/stuck:	مستعصي	accidents:	إصطدام
person:	شخص	personality:	شخصية
see (e):	بص	little light:	بصيص
baldheaded:	أصلع	finger:	إصبع
soap:	صابون	cockroach:	صرصور
glass:	كلاص	onions:	بصل
quail:	عصفور	hush:	هص
prayer:	صلاة	pray (v.):	صلي
he prayed:	صلى	he fasted:	صام
cross:	صليب	patient:	صبور
Friday:	جمعة	Sunday:	أحد
final fate:	مصير	eco:	صدى
statue of pagans:	صنم	correct/true:	صحيح
picture:	صورة	sound:	صوط
half:	نُص	concept:	مصطلح
word root (infinitive form):	مصدر	adjective:	صفة
letter:	حرف	letters:	حروف
consonant:	حرف صحيح	vowel:	حرف علة
vowels:	حروف ألعلة	Herekaat:	حركات
word:	كلمة	sentence:	جملة
these (e):	دُل	this (e) ♀:	ده

The Arabic Alphabet for English Speakers

❸ Practice writing these four shapes of the letter صاد:

صـ ـصـ ـصـ ص
ص ـصـ ـصـ صـ

صاد   مِصْر   شَخَص   باص

صاد صـ صـ صـ صـ   ‎ ‎ ‎ ‎ ‎ ‎ ‎ ‎ ‎ ‎ صـ صـ صـ صـ صـ   ‎ ‎ ‎ ‎ ‎ ‎ ‎ ‎ ‎ مِصْر

شَخص ص ص ص ص   ‎ ‎ ‎ ‎ ‎ ‎ ‎ ‎ ‎ ص ص ص ص ص   ‎ ‎ ‎ ‎ ‎ ‎ ‎ ‎ باص

صا   صو   صي   صاصا   صوصو   صاصو   صيصو

صي   صيصي   صوص   صاص   لاص   باص

صَلْصَة   خاص   خِصوصي   خاصَةً   صاد   مُصطفى

صَدى   بُص   صار   مِصر   شَخص   شَخْصِيَة

لِصوص   بَصيص   صَلاح   ناصِر   صَباح   إصْطِدام

صَيف   مَصيف   حُمْصي   صابون   وارصو   كْلاص

مَصير   مَصدَر   مُصطَلَح   إصْبع   بَصَل   صَحيح

إنْصاف   صاص   صَص   صوص   صُص   صيص

بَصيص   صَرصور   بُص دَه عِصْفور   دَه بَصَل   صِص

صَعبة   شَخصِيَة مِش شَخصِيَة   صار   شَخص صَعب   هُص وبُص دَه لُص

أصلَع   أمور مِستَعصِيَة   دَه مِسْتَوصِف خِصوصي مِش عِمومي

دُل حَرَكات   دَه حَرف عِلَة   دَه حَرف صَحيح   صَبير صَبور

صومال   مَصير شَعب   دَه نُص ونُص   مَصنَع في مَصر

صِ   صي   صُ   صو   صَ   صا   صاد   إصبَع

❹ Pick the correct shape of the letter صاد to fill in these blanks:

ص ص ص ص ص
ص ص ص ص ص

صاد   مِصْر   شَخْص   باص

←

__ا __و __ي __ا __ا __و __ا __و
__ي __و __ي __ي __ي __و __لا
با__ __ة خا__ خِ__و__ي خا__ة __أ__ة __اد
مُ__طفى __دى بُ__ار مِ__ر __شخ__
شَخْ__ِيَة لِ__و__ بَ__ي __لاح نا__ر __باح
إ__طِدام __يف مَ__يف حُمْ__ي __ابون وار__و
كُلا__ مَ__ير مَ__دَر مُ__طَلَح إِ__بَع بَ__ل
__حيح إنْ__اف __و__ __ا__ي __و دَه بَ__ل
بُ__ دَه عِ__فور __رْ__ور بَ__ي__ هُ__ وبُ__ دَه لُ__
شَخْ__ __عب __ار مِش شَخْ__ِيَة __عبة دَه مِسْتَو__ف
خِ__و__ي مِش عِمومي إمور مِستَعــ__ِيَة أ__لَع __ير
__بور دَه حَرف __حيح دَه حَرف عِلة دُل حَرَكات مَ__نَع
في مَ__ر دَه نُ__ وِنُ__ مَ__ير __ومال إ__بَع
__اد __ا __و __ي __ص

Chapter 4 — Z: ظ — Zaa': ظاء

This Arabic letter name has a special sound and in different dialects, it has two different names. It is pronounced like a z: ز in Egyptian dialect and almost like a D: ض in the Gulf region dialect. Therefore, it is called Zaa' ظاء in Egypt and, it called is Daa' in the Gulf region. Usually, if a word is used in the Gulf dialect, it is represented with a "d" in English, as in (Dubai: ظُبَي). However, if it is used in an Egyptian dialect, it is represented with a "z" in English, as in (Naguib Mahfouz: مَحْفوظ نَجيب). In this book its name is Zaa' ظاء. The letter Zaa' ظاء is a consonant and it is given the symbol of the capital "Z" in this book to tell it apart from the ordinary "z." Like the rest of the Arabic letters, the ظاء has four shapes: beginning ظ, middle ظ, end ظ, and isolated ظ. The ظاء is pronounced in two different ways in the Middle East. The ظاء a minor letter because it occurs in approximately 38 words.

ظ ظ ظ ظ

مَحْفوظ   حافُظ   نَظيف   ظاء

❶ Read these Arabic words aloud slowly focusing on the four shapes of Zaa' ظاء:

well kept:	مَحْفوظ	keep/memorize:	إحفِظ
keeper:	حافِظ	conservative:	مُحافِظ
clean:	نظَّف	clean (adj.):	نَظيف
back:	ظَهر	noon:	ظُهر
phenomenon ♀:	ظاهِرَة	apparent:	ظاهِر
appearances:	مُظاهِر	appearance:	مَظهَر
circumstance:	ظِروف	demonstration ♀:	مُظاهَرَة
envelope:	ظَرْف	circumstances:	ظِروف
lucky:	مَحْفوض	envelops:	ظِروف
darkness:	ظَلام	luck:	حَظ
downtrodden:	مَظلوم	autocrat:	ظالِم
weakened:	مُستُظعَف	weak:	ظَعيف
organization ♀:	مُنَظَمَة	weakened ♀:	مُستَضعَفة
employee ♀:	مُوَظَفة	employee:	مُوظَف
sight:	نَظَر	scene:	مَنْظَر
pronounce:	إلْفِظ	pronunciation:	لَفظ
spell for me:	إتْهَجا لي	for me:	لي
		pronounce for me:	إلفِظ لي

The Arabic Alphabet for English Speakers

❷ Read aloud the ظ with other learned letters five times per each page:

ظا ظو ظي ظوظا ظيظو ظاظ ظوظ لظ مظ

هظ نظ جظ سظ تظ فظ كظ ضظ عظ شظ

حظ ثظ خظ صظ دظ وظ رظ زظ ذظ يظ

ياظ دوظ داظ روظ زوظ راظ باظ ماظ لاظ

هاظ نوظ جاظ ساظ شاظ فاظ كاظ عاظ حاظ

خوظ صوظ ظوظ كظت بظو مظي نظح نظج

سظم عظي شظر حظر ثظي خظر صظذ ظاء

ظاهِرَة مَظْهَر ظالِم ظِروف ظَرِف مُوَظَّف

نَظيف حافُظ مَحْفوظ ظَبي لَفظ اِلْفُظ اِنْظِمام نَظَر

مَنْظَر مَظْهَر ظَلام مَظْلوم واعِظ مُحافِظ مُظاهَرَة

حَظ مَحْظوظ حافِظ ظا ظَ ظُ ظِ ظْ

❸ Practice writing these four shapes of the letter ظاء:

ظ ظ ظ ظ

ظ ظ ظ ظ

ظ ظ ظ ظاء _____ نَظَر ظ ظ ظ _____

حَظ ظ ظ ظ ظ _____ مَحْفوظ ظ ظ ظ ظ _____

ظا	ظو	ظي	ظوظا	ظيظو	ظاظ	ظوظ	لظ
مظ	هظ	نظ	جظ	سظ	تظ	فظ	كظ	ضظ
عظ	شظ	حظ	ثظ	خظ	صظ	دظ	وظ	رظ
زظ	ذظ	يظ	ياظ	دوظ	داظ	روظ	راظ	زوظ
باظ	ماظ	لاظ	هاظ	نوظ	جاظ	ساظ	شاظ
فاظ	كاظ	عاظ	حاظ	خوظ	صوظ	ظوظ	كظت
بظو	مظي	نظح	نظج	سظم	عظي	شظر	حظر
ثظي	خظر	صظظذ	ظاء	ظاهِرَة	مَظْهر	ظَهْر
ظالِم	ظِروف	ظَرف	مُوَظَف	نَظيف	حافُظ	مَحْفوظ

ظَلام مَظْهَر مَنْظَر نَظَر إنْظِمام الْفُظ لَفَظ ظَبي

مَحْظوظ حَظ مُظاهَرَة مُحافِظ واعِظ مَظْلوم

عَظيم فَظيع أبو ظَبي ظِنون ظَنْ حافِظ مَحْفوظ

ظْ ظِ ظي ظُ ظو ظَ ظا

> Synonyms and Homonyms:

Sometimes, internal vowels حَرَكات above or below letters حروف can change the meaning of the base of a word. For instance, the base حب can be read as حُب or حَب or حِب. However, one is able to correctly read حب from the context in a sentence. Think of the two English words "meet" and "meat" in this sentence, "I will meet you in the meat market." Imagine someone misspelling the two words like this, "I will meat you in the meet market." You will still understand what the person is trying to write from the context of the sentence. Occasionally, words look and sound exactly alike (homonyms) but have different meanings. For example, Zarf ظَرْف means "an envelope" or "a circumstance," and again readers can tell the difference from its context in a sentence.

📢 Read these (bases of words) without the حَرَكات above or below letters:

well kept:	مَحفوظ	memorize:	إحفظ
keeper:	حافظ	conservative:	محافظ
clean:	نظَّف	clean (adj.):	نظيف
back:	ظهر	noon:	ظُهر
phenomenon ♀:	ظاهرة	apparent:	ظاهر
appearances:	مظاهر	appearance:	مظهر
circumstance:	ظِروف	demonstration ♀:	مظاهرة
envelope:	ظَرْف	circumstances:	ظِروف
lucky:	محفوض	envelops:	ظِروف
darkness:	ظلام	luck:	حظ
downtrodden:	مظلوم	autocrat:	ظالم
weakened:	مستظعف	weak:	ظعيف
organization ♀:	منظمة	weakened ♀:	مستضعفة
employee ♀:	موظفة	employee:	موظف
sight:	نظر	scene:	منظر
pronounce:	إلْفظ	pronunciation:	لفظ
spell for me:	إتهجالي	for me:	لي
		pronounce for me:	إلْفظ لي

❹ Pick the correct shape of the letter ظاء to fill in these blanks. Some of these are not words but sounds or words without the حَرَكات above or below letters. In this learning step we are concerned with learning to write the letters and not the meaning of the words. The meaning of words is in the other book entitled *Spoken Arabic for English Speakers by Camilia Sadik*:

ظ   ظ   ظ   ظ

←

__ا   __و__   __ي   __و__ا   __و__يـ__و   __ا__

__و   __ل__   __مـ__   __هـ__   __نـ__   __جـ__   __سـ__ت   __ت

__ف   __ك   __ضـ__   __عـ__   __شـ__   __حـ__   __ثـ__   __خ

__صـ__   __د__   __و__   __ر__   __ز__   __ذ__   __يـ__   __يا

دو__   دا__   رو__   را__   زو__   با__   ما__   لا__

ها__   نو__   جا__   سا__   شا__   فا__   كا__

عا__   حا__   خو__   صو__   __و__   كـ__ت

بـ__و   مـ__ي   نـ__حـ__   نـ__جـ__   سـ__م   عـ__ي

شـ__ر   حـ__ر   ثـ__ي   خـ__ر   صـ__ذ   __اء

__اهِرَة   مَ__هَر   __هْر   __الِم   __روف   __رِف

مُوَ__ف   نَ__يف   حافُ__   مَحْفو__   __بي   لَ__ف

__الْفُ__   إنْ__مام   نَ__ر   مَنْ__ر   مَ__هَر   __اهِر

__لام   __لِمَة   مَ__لوم   مُحافِ__   مُ__اهَرَة   حَ__

مَحْ__و__   حافِ__   __نْ__   __نون   أبو__

__بي   فَ__يع   كا__م

169

Chapter 5 — gh: غ — gheyn: غَين

This Arabic letter name is gheyn غَين and it has a special sound– just like the French "r." In English, the غَين is often represented with a "gh" as in (Afghanistan: 'ef·ghaa·nis·taan أَفْغانِسْتان). The letter غَين is a consonant and it is given the symbol "gh" in this book. The غَين has four shapes: beginning غ‍, middle ‍غ‍, end ‍غ, and isolated غ:

غ	‍غ	‍غ‍	غ‍
بْراغ	بالِغ	بَغْداد	غَين

❶ Read these Arabic words aloud slowly focusing on the four shapes of غَين:

Afghanistan:	'ef·ghaa'·nis·taan	أَفغانِستان
Baghdad:	begh·daad'	بَغداد
gas:	ghaaz	غاز
gram:	ghraam	غْرام
telegram:	tel·ghraam'	تَلغْرام
deer/gazelle:	ghe·zaal'	غَزال
Prague:	braagh	بْراغ
Belgrade:	belgh·raad'	بَلغْراد
Guatemala:	ghwaa'·tee·maa·leh	غواتيمالَة
Singapore:	sin·ghaa'·foor	سِنغافور
Uruguay:	'oo·righ·waay'	أورِغواي
Gaza:	ghe·'zeh	غَزَة
Morocco:	megh'·rib	مَغرِب
cracked wheat:	bur'·ghul	بُرغُل
lamb:	leHm ghe'·nem	لَحم غَنَم
sunset:	ghi roob'	غِروب
he crafted:	صاغ	he crafts:	يَصيغ
craft (v.):	صيغ	crafted:	مَصيوغ
winner:	غالِب	loser:	مَغلوب
manipulating:	مُراوَغَة	manipulator:	مُراوِغ

170

a wish:	رَغبَة	wrong:	غَلَط
brain:	دَماغ	my brain:	دماغي
cheating:	غِش	tomorrow:	غَداً
song:	أُغنية	songs	أغاني
sing:	غَني	I sing:	أغني
naïve:	غَشيم	stupid:	غبي
empty:	فارغ	expensive:	غالي
painter, not artist:	صَبّاغ	boil (v.):	إغلي
change (v.):	غَيِّر	other:	غَير
language:	لُغَة	the language:	أَلْلُغة
gossip:	لَغوَة	work (n.):	شُغل
washer:	غَسالة	dryer:	مُيَبِسة
laundry:	غَسيل	wash (v.):	إغسِل
I wash:	أغسِل	he washes:	يَغسِل
she washes ♀:	تَغسِل	we wash:	نَغسِل
they wash:	يَغسِلون	I'll wash:	سأغسِل
contraction of the verb will: prefix **se**			سَ
he'll wash:	سَيَغسِل	she'll wash:	سَتَغسِل
we'll wash:	سَنَغسِل	they'll wash:	سَيَغسِلون
exaggeration:	مُبالَغة	exaggerate:	بالِغ
I exaggerate:	أبالِغ	he exaggerates:	يُبالِغ
she exaggerates:	تُبالِغ	we exaggerate:	نُبالِغ
they exaggerate:	يُبالِغون	I'll exaggerate:	سأبالِغ
he'll exaggerate:	سَيُبالِغ	she'll exaggerate:	سَتُبالِغ
we'll exaggerate:	سَنُبالِغ	they'll exaggerate:	سَيبالِغون

The Arabic Alphabet for English Speakers

❷ Read aloud the غ with other learned letters five times per each page:

←

غاغر غيغ غيغي غيغو غي غوغ غا

بُرغُل غَزال غَنَم غالي دَماغي واغي غاغي

غَني غين بِلوغ رَغبَة مو غَبي غشيم أورِغواي

غَير غَشاش مِش غِش أَغاني أُغنِيَة غَلَط غرام أغنى

أفغانِستان تَلِغرام شُغل أَلْغَسالَة غَسيل إغلي غَيِّر

مُبالَغة أَلْلُغَة لَغوَة لُغَة مَغرِب بَغْداد بَلِغراد سِنغافور

صاغ يَصيغ صيغ سَيُبالِغون يُبالِغ أبالِغ بالِغ بَغيض

غِروب مُراوَغة صَبّاغ فارِغ سَأغْسِل يَغسِلون يَغسِل

غَسان غادَة مَغرور غِرور بَغيض مَغلوب غالِب

مُغْلَق مَغارَة مَغول مَغزى مَغَص غَوّاصة غوريلا

غَيث تَغليف تَغيير تَغَيَّر جُغرافيا شَغَف نَغَم شُغل

غِ غُ غَ غَين تَغلُب يَغار غار صَغير كَغْم ثَغرَة

**Read the words from above (bases of words) without the حَرَكات above or below the letters:

Afghanistan:	ʼef·ghaaʼ·nis·taan	أفغانستان
Baghdad:	begh·daadʼ	بغداد
gas:	ghaaz	غاز
gram:	ghraam	غرام
telegram:	tel·ghraamʼ	تلغرام
deer/gazelle:	ghe·zaalʼ	غزال
Prague:	braagh	براغ
Belgrade:	belgh·raadʼ	بلغراد
Guatemala:	ghwaaʼ·tee·maa·laa	غواتيمالا
Singapore:	sin·ghaaʼ·foor	سنغافور
Uruguay:	ʼoo·righ·waayʼ	أورغواي
Gaza:	gheˑʼzeh	غزة
Morocco:	meghʼ·rib	مغرب
cracked wheat:	burʼ·ghul	برغل
lamb:	leHm gheʼ·nem	لحم غنم
sunset:	ghi roobʼ	غروب

he crafted:	صاغ	he crafts:	يصيغ
craft (v.):	صيغ	crafted:	مصيوغ
winner:	غالب	loser:	مغلوب
manipulating:	مراوغة	manipulator:	مراوغ
a wish:	رغبة	wrong:	غلط
brain:	دماغ	my brain:	دماغي
cheating:	غش	tomorrow:	غدا
song:	أُغنية	songs	أغاني
sing:	غني	I sing:	أغني

naïve:	غشيم	stupid:	غبي
empty:	فارغ	expensive:	غالي
painter, not artist:	صباغ	boil (v.):	إغلي
change (v.):	غَيِّر	other:	غير
language:	لُغَة	the language:	اَلْلُغة
gossip:	لغوة	work (n.):	شغل
washer:	غسالة	dryer:	ميبسة
laundry:	غسيل	wash (v.):	إغسل
I wash:	أغسل	he washes:	يغسل
she washes ♀:	تغسل	we wash:	نغسل
they wash:	يغسلون	I'll wash:	سأغسل
contraction of the verb will:		prefix **se**	سَـ
he'll wash:	سيغسل	she'll wash:	ستغسل
we'll wash:	سنغسل	they'll wash:	سيغسلون
exaggeration:	مبالغة	exaggerate:	بالغ
I exaggerate:	أبالغ	he exaggerates:	يبالغ
she exaggerates:	تبالغ	we exaggerate:	نبالغ
they exaggerate:	يبالغون	I'll exaggerate:	سأبالغ
he'll exaggerate:	سيبالغ	she'll exaggerate:	ستبالغ
we'll exaggerate:	سنبالغ	they'll exaggerate:	سيبالغون

The Arabic Alphabet for English Speakers

❸ Practice writing these four shapes of the letter غَين:

غين غ غ غ غـ ـغـ ـغـ ـغـ ـغ لُغَة

بَغْداد غـ غـ غـ غـ غـ بْراغ

غا غو غوغ غيغي غيغو غي غيغي غاغِر

غاغي واغي دَماغي غاز غالي غَنَم غَزال بُرغُل

أورغواي موغبي غشيم رَغبَة بلوغ غين غَنِي

أغني غرام غَلَط أُغنِيَة أغاني غِش مِش غَشّاش غير

غَيَّر إغلي غَسيل ألغَسّالَة شُغل تَلِغرام أفغانِستان

سِنغافور بلغراد بَغْداد مَغرِب لُغَة لَغوَة ألّلُغَة مُبالَغَة

يَغْسِل يَغْسِلون سَأغْسِل فارغ صَبّاغ مُراوغَة غُروب

غالِب مَغلوب بَغيض غرور مَغرور غادَة غَسّان

غوريلا غَوّاصَة مَغَص مَغزى مَغول مَغارَة مُغلَق

شُغل نَغَم شَغَف جُغرافيا تَغيير تَغيير تَغليف غَيث

ثَغرَة كَغَم صَغير غار يَغار تَغلُب غين غَ غُ غِ

The Arabic Alphabet for English Speakers

❹ Pick the correct shape of the letter غَين to fill in these blanks:

غ ـغ ـغـ غـ
غ ـغ ـغـ غـ

←

ـــا ـــو ـــو ـــيـ ـــي ـــيـ ـــو ـــو ـــا ـــ

ـــي واـــي ـــا ـــي ـــا ـــر ـــا ـــيـ ـــي ـــي

بُرـــل ـــزال ـــنَم ـــالي ـــاز ـــي دَما ـــي

ـــين بلو ـــبَة رَـــبَة موـــبي ـــشيم ـــواي أورِ

أـــاني ـــنِية لـــط ـــرام ـــنى أـــني

ـــسيل ـــلي إـــير ـــيّر ـــير شاش مِش ـــش

ـــافور سِنـــ أفـــانِستان تَلِـــرام شُـــل أَلـــسالَة

ألـــة لـــوة لـــة مـــرب بـــداد ـــراد بِـــ

سَيُبالِـــون يُبالِـــ أبالِـــ بالِـــ بَـــيض مُبالـــة

سَأـــسِل يَـــسِلون يَـــسِل صا ـــيصي صي

مَـــلوب ـــالِب ـــروب مُراوـــة صبّاـــ فارِ

ـــوريلا ـــسان ـــادة مَـــرور ـــرور بَـــيض

مَـــارَة مَـــول مَـــزى مَـــص ـــواصِة

تَـــيّر جُـــرافيا شَـــف نَـــم شُـــل مُـــلَق

صَـــير كَـــم ثَـــرَة ـــيث تَـــليف تَـــيير

ـــار يَـــار تَـــلُب أنا فِعلاً مِن بَـــداد حَبيبَتي.

Chapter 6 — ق q: qaaf قاف

This Arabic letter name is qaaf قاف and it has a special sound that is like the English "k." The letter qaaf قاف is a consonant and it is given the symbol "q" in this book. The قاف is often represented with "k" or "q" in English, as in (Iraq: Ai·raaq عِراق), and as in (music: mōo·see'·qaw موسيقى). The letter قاف has four shapes: beginning ق, middle ـقـ, end ـق, and isolated ق:

ق   ـقـ   ـق   ق

قاف   موسيقى   صَديق   عِراق

❶ Read these Arabic words aloud slowly focusing on the four shapes of قاف:

Iraq:	عِراق	music:	موسيقى
neck:	رَقَبَة	democracy:	ديموقراطِيَة
beqlaaweh:	بَقلاوَة	'elif meqSooreh:	ألِف مَقصورة
bugs:	بَق	cotton:	قُطن
Kabul:	قابول	Cairo:	ألْقاهِرَة
Cordoba:	قُرطُبَة	Cypress:	قُبرُص
Madagascar:	مَدَغَشقَر	Area/Region:	مَنطَقَة
market:	سوق	hotel:	فُندُق
say:	قول	drive:	سوق
I drive:	أَسوق	he drives:	يَسوق
dictionary:	قاموس	pen:	قَلَم
box:	صَندوق	lock:	قِفل
scissors:	مَقَص	teapot:	قوري
coffee:	قَهوَة	coffee shop:	مَقهى
friend:	صَديق	honest:	صادِق
reading:	قِراءة	I read:	أَقرَأ
he reads:	يَقرَأ	get up:	قوم
Socrates:	سُقراط	discussion:	مُناقَشَة
energy:	طاقَة	old/ancient:	قَديم

little:	قَليل	trivial:	حَقير
short:	قَصير	narrow/tight:	ضَيِّق
ugly:	قَبيح	giant:	عَملاق
blue:	أزرَق	dark blue:	أزرَق غامِق
orange:	بُرتَقالي	oranges:	بُرتَقال
blond:	أشقَر	well-read:	قاريء جَيد
time:	وَقت	stop (v.):	قِف
The east:	ألْشَرق	The Middle East:	ألْشرق ألأوسَط

The Arabic Alphabet for English Speakers

❷ Read aloud the ق with all the learned letters, five times per each page:

قَا قاق قو قوق قي قيق قَق قُق قِق واقي قول

يَقول قوم قُبرُص قاموس قَهوَة قوري قوزي قَليل

يَقرأ قِراءَة قَديم قُطن طاقَة بَقلاوَة مَنطَقَة مَقَص

مَقهى سُقراط لقلق أَشْقَر بُرتَقال صَديق بَق

ديمُقراطيَة ضَيِّق غامِق ألْعِراق سوق فُندُق صَندوق

عِملاق بوق ألْشَرق ألْأَوْسَط ألف مَقْصورَة قلب عالِق

في الْخاتِمَة أقول مَبروك عَليكُم جِهودي فَترَة عَشر سِنوات وَأنا أغور في اَللغة اَلْعَرَبِيَة وَأفِكِكَها واكْتَشِف ثُم أكتِب لَكُم هذا إِلْكِتاب اَلْثَمين. في اَلْحَقيقَة، أصْل سيبَوَيه من بِلاد اَلْرافِدَين اَلتي هِيَ بِلادي، وَقد كان سيبَوَيه لا يَتَكَلَّم اَلْعَرَبِية جيداً وضَحَكوا عَلَيه حينَ كان يَتَكَلَّم، فقَرَر أَنْ يَغور في اَللغة اَلْعَرَبِيَة وَفَكَكَها وَدَوَّن قَواعِدها. إِنَّ سيبَوَيه جِدي لُغَوِياً وَأنا حفيدَتُه. مَحَبَّتي وَتَقْديري لِلْجَميع، كاميليا صادِق.

Read these words (bases of words) without the حَرَكات above or below letters:

Iraq:	عراق	music:	موسيقى
beqlaaweh:	بقلاوة	neck:	رقبة
bugs:	بق	cotton:	قطن
Kabul:	قابول	Cairo:	ألقاهرة
Cordoba:	قرطبة	Cypress:	قبرص
Madagascar:	مدغشقر	Area/Region:	منطقة
market:	سوق	hotel:	فندق
say:	قول	drive:	سوق
I drive:	أسوق	he drives:	يسوق
dictionary:	قاموس	pen:	قلم
box:	صندوق	lock:	قفل
scissors:	مقص	teapot:	قوري
coffee:	قهوة	coffee shop:	مقهى
friend:	صديق	honest:	صادق
reading:	قراءة	I read:	أقرأ
he reads:	يقرأ	get up:	قوم
Socrates:	سقراط	discussion:	مناقشة
energy:	طاقة	old/ancient:	قديم
little:	قليل	trivial:	حقير
short:	قصير	narrow/tight:	ضَيِّق
ugly:	قبيح	giant:	عملاق
blue:	أزرق	dark blue:	أزرق غامق
orange:	برتقالي	oranges:	برتقال
blond:	أشقر	well-read:	قاريء جيد
time:	وقت	stop (v.):	قف

The Arabic Alphabet for English Speakers

❸ Practice writing these four shapes of the letter قاف:

ق ـقـ ـق ق
ق ـقـ ـق ق

قاف   موسيقى   صَديق   عِراق

قا   قاق   قو   قوق   قي   قيق   فَق   قُق   قِق   واقي   قول

بَقول   قوم   قُبرُص   قاموس   قَهوَة   قوري   قوزي   قَليل

يَقرأ   قِراءَة   قَديم   قُطن   طاقَة   بَقلاوَة   مَنطَقَة   مَقَص

مَقهى   سُقراط   لقلق   أشْقَر   بُرتَقال   صَديق   بَق

ديمُقراطيَة   ضَيِّق   غامِق   العِراق   سوق   فُندُق   صَندوق

صادِق   عِملاق   بوق   الشَرق الأوسَط   ألف مَقصورَة   قلب

عالِق   في الخاتِمَة أقول مَبروك عَليكُم جهودي فَترَة خَمْس سِنوات وَأنا

أغور في اللغَة العَرَبية وَأفَكِكَها وَاكتَشِف ثُم أكتِب لَكُم هذا الكِتاب الثَمين.

مَحَبَتي وَتَقْديري لِلجَميع.

❹ Pick the correct shape of the letter قاف to fill in these blanks:

ق ـق ـقـ قـ
ق ـق ـقـ قـ

قاف   موسيقى   صَديق   عِراق

←

_ـا_   _ـا_   _ـو_   _ـي_   _ـي_   وا_ي

_هوَة   _اموس   _بِرُص   _وم   يَ_ول   _ول

_ديم   _راءَة   يَ_رأ   _ليل   _وزي   _وري

مَ_هى   مَ_ص   منطَ_ة   بَ_لاوَة   طا_ة   _طن

بَ_   صَديـ_   بُرتَ_ال   أشْ_ر   لـ_لـ_   سُ_راط

قُندُ_   سو_   ألْعِرا_   غامِ_   ضَيِّ_   ديمُ_راطيَة

_ عالـ_   _لب   بو_   عِملا_   صادِ_   صَندو_

تَ_ديري   أ_ول   مَ_صورَة   ألف مَ_   ألأوْسَط   ألشَر_

Rules to divide Arabic Words into Syllables
كيفية تَقْسيم الكَلِمات إلى مَقاطِع

Understanding Diphthongs:

A diphthong is a condition whereby two or more vowels in a syllable produce a single sound. We know that two sounding vowels cannot exist in a syllable. If more than one vowel exists in a single syllable, only a single sound can be heard. This condition is true both in Arabic and in English. For instance, we only hear the single sound of "u" in "eau" in "b*eau*·ti·ful," and we only hear one sound in the "au" is "auto." English is filled with examples of diphthongs and so is Arabic. Because two sounding vowels cannot exist in one syllable, the other vowel/s in that same syllable must become either silent or they must change to a "y" or a "w". When that change occurs, it is called a diphthong.

This is what happens in Arabic when more than one vowel exists in a syllable:

(1) Two sounding vowels next to each other split forming two independent syllables:

a question: soo·aal	سؤآل	Zaire: zaa·'eer	زائير
reading: qi·raa·'eh	قِراءَة	Raul: raa·'ooool	راؤول

(2) One vowel in a syllable has a sound and the rest of the vowel/s are silent:

I: *aa*'e·n*aa*	أنا	I bring: *aa*'e·jeeb	أجيب
food: *aa*'ekl	أكْل	Alaska: *aa*'e·laas·kaa	ألاسْكا
mother: *aa*'um	أم	English: *aa*'in·ki·lee·zee	إنْكِليزي
to: *aa*'i·law	إلى	Orlando: *aa*'oor·laan·doo	أورلانْدو
aa'ook·laa·hoo·maa	أوكِلاهوما	Raul: raa·'*oo*ool	راؤول
problem: mes·*aa*'e·leh	مُشْكِلَة	responsible: mes·*oo*'ool	مَسؤول
thanks: shuk·r*aa*en	شُكْراً	you welcome: Aef·w*aa*en	عَفْواً
very: ji·d*aa*en	جِداً	a lot: ke·thee·r*aa*en	كَثيراً
always: daa·'i·m*aa*en	دائماً	nighttime: lay·l*aa*en	لَيْلاً
a little: qa·lee·l*aa*en	قَليلاً	first of all: '*aa*ew·we·l*aa*an	أوَلاً

(3) One vowel has a sound and the other turns to a "y" or a "w" in one syllable as in:

toilet: ti·waa·leyt	توالَيْت	Vegas: fey·kes	فَيْكَس
Beirut: bey·root	بَيْروت	lemons: ley·moon	لَيْمون
Kuwait: kew·weyt	كُوَيْت	Taiwan: taay·waan	تايْوان
Troy: troy	ثروي	sound: sewt	صَوْت
tea: shaay	شاي	zaay:	زاي

Rules for dividing words into syllables: The absolute rule is not to have two sounding vowels in one syllable. The general rule is to divide between two consonants as in war·deh and bey·root. However, don't divide a consonant blend like the "lm" in film. The other general rule is to divide after a vowel (before a consonant) as in Ae·re·bee, ri·baaT, and bu·Tul. This book has all the words divided into syllables to help you get started. Pay attention to the patterns in which words are divided into syllables in this book.

Practice Test of Part Five

Translate these words and sounds into Arabic letters:

thaa'	thaanee	ketheer	Hedeeth	turaath
khaakee	'ekh	mekhbez	meTbekh	baakh
Saar	'elqaahireh	shekhS	baaS	ZeAeef
neZeef	HaafiZ	meHfooZ	mish	beghdaad
yubaaligh	braagh	qaamoos	mooseeqaw	Sedeeq
Airaaq	qif	thelj	ketheer	turaath
thaalith	judith	meTbekh	kherdel	khookh
khudh	mustewSif	SeAeb	beSel	SeHeeH
waaHid	jumleh	kelimeh	Zuhr	meHZooZ
muweZef	niZaal	AeZeem	ZeAeef	efghaanistaan
keeloo	ghraam	ghezeh	singhaafoor	meghrib
ghezaal	burghul	leHm ghenem	ghenee	lugheh
gheseel	'ighsil	seneghsil	mōoseeqaw	deemuqraaTiyeh
beqlaawaa	quTn	'elqaahireh	qubruS	qaabool
beq	menTeqeh	sooq	ghirnaaTeh	qurTubeh
findiq	qool	qifl	Sendooq	qooree
qehweh	meqhaw	qiraa'eh	qoom	suqraaT
munaaqesheh	'ezreq	burteqaal	'eshqer	'elsherq 'elewSeT
daa'imen	medreseh	'enaa	'illee	'edrus

'eyweh	li'enehu	'ewelen	laazim	hiye
huwe	nereed	nehr 'elneel	'ilyoom	beeyaanoo
doolaar	bidoon	'elshaay	'eswed	'ew bibsee
weyn	'elsooq	'elăn	hinaa	yelleh 'imshee
jemeel	ledheedh	TebAen	werdeh	'ellugheh
'elAerebiyeh	'el'inkileeziyeh	'eldiwel	lubnaan	sooriyeh
'el'urdun	feleSteen	'elAiraaq	'elkuweyt	'elsiAoodiyeh
'elbeHreyn	Aumaan	'el'imaaraat	'elyemen	miSr
leebyeh	toonis	'eljezaa'ir	'elmeghrib	'elsoodaan

➤The True Order of the Arabic Alphabet:
Changing the order of presenting the Arabic alphabet was necessary; however, this is the actual order of the Arabic alphabet:

ا ب ت ث ج ح خ د ذ ر ز س ش

ص ض ط ظ ع غ ف ق ك ل م ن ه و ي

Chart of the Learned Letters & Symbols and their Shapes

Letter Name	Symbol as in	Isolated	End	Middle	Beginning
'elif	aa: father	ا	ـا		ا
baa'	b: bank	ب	ـب	ـبـ	بـ
taa'	t: tub	ت	ـت	ـتـ	تـ
thaa'	th: math	ث	ـث	ـثـ	ثـ
jeem	j: jet	ج	ـج	ـجـ	جـ
Haa'	H: Hebibi	ح	ـح	ـحـ	حـ
khaa'	kh: Bach	خ	ـخ	ـخـ	خـ
daal	d: dip	د	ـد		د
dhaal	dh: that	ذ	ـذ		ذ
raa'	r: radio	ر	ـر		ر
zaay	z: zoo	ز	ـز		ز
seen	s: sit	س	ـس	ـسـ	سـ
sheen	sh: ship	ش	ـش	ـشـ	شـ
Saad	S: sum	ص	ـص	ـصـ	صـ
Daad	D: Riyaadh	ض	ـض	ـضـ	ضـ
Taa'	T: kilowatt	ط	ـط	ـطـ	طـ
Zaa'	Z: Mahfouz	ظ	ـظ	ـظـ	ظـ
Aeyn	A: Arabic	ع	ـع	ـعـ	عـ
gheyn	gh: Brach	غ	ـغ	ـغـ	غـ
faa'	f: fill	ف	ـف	ـفـ	فـ
qaaf	q: Iraq	ق	ـق	ـقـ	قـ
kaaf	k: kit	ك	ـك	ـكـ	كـ
laam	l: until	ل	ـل	ـلـ	لـ
meem	m: may	م	ـم	ـمـ	مـ
noon	n: noon	ن	ـن	ـنـ	نـ
haa'	h: his	ه	ـه	ـهـ	هـ
waaw: w or oo	w: will oo: boot	و	ـو	ـو	و
yaa': y or ee	y: you ee: meet	ي	ـي	ـيـ	يـ
hemzeh	': Sinai'	ء			
'elif meqSooreh	aw: law	ى	ـى		
meddeh	ă/aa: man	آ			
fetHeh	e: set	َ			
Demmeh	u: put	ُ			
kesreh	i: sit or ski	ِ			
sekoon	consonant blend	ْ			
sheddeh	double letters	ّ			

www.ingramcontent.com/pod-product-compliance
Lightning Source LLC
Chambersburg PA
CBHW060421010526
44118CB00017B/2307